Visual Analytics
Fundamentals

Visual Analytics Fundamentals

Creating Compelling Data Narratives with Tableau

Lindy Ryan

✦Addison-Wesley

Boston • Columbus • New York • San Francisco • Amsterdam •
Cape Town • Dubai • London • Madrid • Milan • Munich •
Paris • Montreal • Toronto • Delhi • Mexico City • São Paulo •
Sydney • Hong Kong • Seoul • Singapore • Taipei • Tokyo

Figure Credits

Pearson's Commitment to Diversity, Equity, and Inclusion

Pearson is dedicated to creating bias-free content that reflects the diversity of all learners. We embrace the many dimensions of diversity, including but not limited to race, ethnicity, gender, socioeconomic status, ability, age, sexual orientation, and religious or political beliefs.

Education is a powerful force for equity and change in our world. It has the potential to deliver opportunities that improve lives and enable economic mobility. As we work with authors to create content for every product and service, we acknowledge our responsibility to demonstrate inclusivity and incorporate diverse scholarship so that everyone can achieve their potential through learning. As the world's leading learning company, we have a duty to help drive change and live up to our purpose to help more people create a better life for themselves and to create a better world.

Our ambition is to purposefully contribute to a world where

- Everyone has an equitable and lifelong opportunity to succeed through learning.
- Our educational products and services are inclusive and represent the rich diversity of learners.
- Our educational content accurately reflects the histories and experiences of the learners we serve.
- Our educational content prompts deeper discussions with learners and motivates them to expand their own learning (and worldview).

While we work hard to present unbiased content, we want to hear from you about any concerns or needs with this Pearson product so that we can investigate and address them.

Please contact us with concerns about any potential bias at https://www.pearson.com/report-bias.html.

Contents at a Glance

Contents

PREFACE

For as long as I can remember, I have always been fascinated by the power of a good story.

Like taste buds, our taste for stories evolves over time, both in terms of format and content. Our appetite changes alongside age, experiences, and interests, yet still the desire for a good story persists. We crave stories; it's part of our design. Humans are intrinsically hungry for a good story. They entertain us, educate us, and provide mechanisms to transmit knowledge, information, and experiences. We're rather indiscriminate about how we receive stories, too. In fact, according to scientific evidence, we might even *prefer* stories that move us and touch our senses.

So it is with data stories. As we learn to communicate the results of our analysis—the hidden secrets carefully plucked from within the rows and columns of our data and curated into insight—we mature from being okay with being told something to wanting to see it for ourselves and, eventually, to wanting to interact with it. We need more information, more context, more action, more substance. This is where visual analytics and visual data storytelling can help.

Today, visual analytics and data storytelling are reshaping how we see, interpret, and communicate data insights. Students from grade school to graduate school are working hands-on with data and changing the way they learn about and communicate about information. Business analysts, managers, and executives are moving away from static, statistic-laden reports and toward interactive, visual data dashboards. Journalists and news editors are using data storyboards and engaging, often interactive, infographics to share information with society-at-large.

Visual analytics helps us visually explore and uncover insights in our data. Data visualization provides a way to showcase our findings by harnessing our brains' visual processing horsepower. Data storytelling gives us a very human way to communicate. This approach pushes beyond the boundaries of simply analyzing information to providing the capacity to communicate it in ways that leave a meaningful, lasting impact.

Together, these converge into what I've termed the "visual imperative," a paradigm shift that has radically reshaped how we work with and seek to understand our data, big and small. This visual imperative is reforming our expectations of information, changing the question from "what can we do with our data" to "what can our data do for us." It's making its mark on every aspect of a progressively data-driven culture, too. From traditional business intelligence and data discovery to the personal analytics on our smart devices to how creators use data to cook up our new favorite television shows, we are becoming more data-dependent and data-driven—and we're doing it *visually*.

While visual analytics and data storytelling leverages some of our innate human communication and knowledge-sharing capabilities, it isn't always an intuitive and obvious process. It takes work, it takes understanding, and it takes a lot of practice. This book is a steppingstone in your journey to becoming a visual analyst, providing the fundamental knowledge and hands-on training needed to help you take your first steps as a visual data storyteller.

Three Core Takeaways

This book focuses on giving you the foundational knowledge, contextualized learning, and hands-on skills you need to be successful in leveraging the power of visual analytics in data visualization and data stories. The goal is not to inundate you with academic lessons in the science of data visualization or story composition, nor to provide a full-scale training experience on any software or technical application, but to provide guidance as you build the necessary skills to visually analyze and represent your data's insights. Therefore, this book concentrates on helping you learn how to organize your data and structure analysis with stories in mind; to embrace exploration and the visual discovery process; and to articulate your findings with rich data, purposefully curated visualizations, and skillfully crafted narrative frameworks. Ultimately, these presentations can help you to deliver your business message while satisfying the needs of your audience. By the time you've reached the end of the text, the expectation is that you will have earned the three core takeaways represented in Figure P.1.

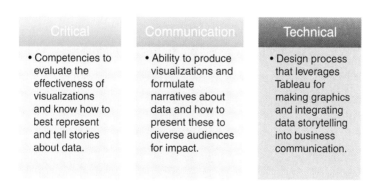

Critical	Communication	Technical
• Competencies to evaluate the effectiveness of visualizations and know how to best represent and tell stories about data.	• Ability to produce visualizations and formulate narratives about data and how to present these to diverse audiences for impact.	• Design process that leverages Tableau for making graphics and integrating data storytelling into business communication.

Figure P.1 The core takeaways.

What You'll Learn in This Book

In visual analytics and data visualization-related courses, students learn how to present data in visual form. This involves working with data, learning how to apply visual design principles, and, often, learning new software. This book will tackle all three. You will learn the following:

- Why we use visual analytics to tell stories about data
- The difference between data visualization for analysis versus presentation
- The fundamentals of visual analytics—from data prep to presentation
- How to design visual analytic outputs that communicate insights and make an impact
- How to create important data visualizations in Tableau and know which to use
- How to utilize concepts of design in data visualization and storytelling
- How to best storyboard your story for your message based on your audience
- How to direct your audience's attention to the most important parts of your data story
- How to design effective business presentations to showcase your data story with Tableau

Who This Book Is For

This book is for anyone who has data and wants to use it to visually communicate its insights to someone else in engaging and memorable ways. This includes, but is not limited to

- Analysts sharing the results of their data discovery or visual analysis
- Students communicating data for reports or presentations
- Teachers helping learners (of any age) to cultivate visual data literacy
- Executives and business managers reporting data-driven results or metrics
- Journalists giving data the starring role in their editorials

Essentially, if you have some data and want to tell a story about it using visualization, then this book is for you. So, from the savviest of data users to students just beginning to learn about the power of data visualization in business communication, if you are interested in becoming a better visual data analyst, curator, and storyteller, then you're in the right place!

There are no prerequisites for this book. In fact, it might be preferable if you're coming into this text with fresh eyes and a fresh perspective. We start with the basics and build incrementally on concepts and to move through the data storytelling process from beginning to end.

Don't let the topic overwhelm you: Whether you have been practicing data visualization and visual analysis for some time or are just taking your first steps in visual analytics, you don't have to be a statistician or a computer scientist, a graphic designer, or even a well-trained writer to learn how to navigate the art and science that is data visualization or to become a master data storyteller. Likewise, you do not need to be a data visualization expert or come armed with deep technical expertise in visualization software packages. Although this book utilizes Tableau as the primary mechanism for data visualization, you need not be a power user or expert prior to getting started— you don't even have to have a purchased license on your machine! You can simply download a free trial of Tableau Desktop to get started. Finally, you don't even need to bring your own data to play just yet (although you certainly can). The sample datasets used in this text, as well as information on where you can find other free datasets, are available to you through the resources listed at the end of this book. Tableau also provides a large selection of sample datasets that you can use for practice, too.

I realize that the idea of visual analysis or data storytelling might sound intimidating to many and that learning new software is always a challenge. Therefore, this book is designed in a way that a professor or a tutor might teach visual data storytelling (and in fact is the approach I take in my classrooms for graduate-level students) using what I call the 1-2-3 Method (see Figure P.2). This breaks down like this: (1) grounding easy-to-understand principles, (2) reinforcing these through real-world examples, and (3) guided hands-on work to incrementally develop skills. By the time you have worked your way through each of the chapters and exercises in this book, you will walk away with something tangible: competency as a visual data storyteller using your own data in your own dashboards and presentations. And you'll have some great visuals on your Tableau Public profile that you can add to your resume!

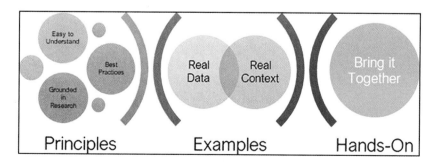

Figure P.2 The 1-2-3 Method

Assumptions

To write a comprehensive text on any of the topics covered in this book would take several volumes and the combined mind power of multiple subject matter experts and scholars across industry and academia. Thus, this book makes some assumptions about the skillset, expectations, and needs of its audience to limit the scope to the most valuable content. My goal is to distill complex topics to the most effective level of detail necessary to help you learn how to leverage visual analytics fundamentals to communicate business-relevant implications using fundamental data visualization and storytelling capabilities of Tableau.

First, this book is focused primarily on fundamentals and is limited in scope to surface-level exploration of various core concepts important to visual data analysis and outputs of visualization and storytelling. While analysis is an intrinsic part of this, in this book you work from a perspective of communicating insights rather than statistical analysis. Thus, the way you curate visualizations for storytelling purposes may be slightly different than how you would approach these tasks if you were designing analytically accurate data representation not intended for presentation. Additionally, while I will touch on subjects like data preparation and wrangling tasks associated with getting data ready for analysis, the full scope of what is involved in all the steps necessary to transform raw data into a workable format is beyond what is covered in this book.

Last, but not least, this book assumes that the reader has access to Tableau Desktop 2022, which is currently available to install on either Windows or Mac operating systems. Free trials are available for business users or general audiences, while students and educators can take advantage of the Tableau for Teaching program, which offers free licenses to the full desktop version.

> A Caveat Versions of Tableau prior to version 2022 support much of the same functionality that you will see in this book. However, the interface is notably different and may affect navigability of instructions in this text.

Why Tableau?

If you browse the shelves of your local bookstore, you'll find a bevy of wonderful books available that teach data visualization and data storytelling in a tool-agnostic manner. There is a good reason for this. To borrow the words of Cole Nussbaumer

Knaflic, author of *Storytelling with Data*, "No matter how good the tool, it will never know your data or its story like you do." With any software, there will always be weak points to balance out the strong ones. However, my goal in this book is to not only give you the information you need but the application to use it. For that, we need a tool.

Many software packages are available on the market that would serve as capable platforms to support this book, including Excel, which is still the most ubiquitous, if unexciting, analysis tool, with the capability to create functional if problematic basic charts and graphs. However, although many of the more advanced available technologies meet the rigors of building beautiful data visualizations, few provide the end-to-end capabilities that Tableau does. What we're looking for is a best-of-breed tool that delivers an approachable, intuitive environment for self-service users of all levels to prepare, analyze, and visualize data, as well as delivery platforms like dashboards and story preparation—and one at the top of employer's wishlist for incoming visual analysts (we'll look at this data in a future chapter). All of these are native to Tableau.

Today, Tableau is the world's leading data visualization analytics software company with over 80,000 customer accounts ranging from small to large organizations across all industries and with users logging on all over the world. Tableau provides a suite of licensed and free software products and excels at displaying data visually, using a drag-and-drop canvas on top of embedded analytics to help users explore their data. As you'll soon see, although Tableau can mimic Excel by providing the capability to analyze rows and columns of numbers, its focus is on interactive, visual data exploration through complex analytical capabilities as well as dashboarding and storytelling features not found in other tools. For more advanced users, Tableau supports a complete formula language and robust data connections: Tableau's live query engine enables users to connect to more than forty different data sources; its in-memory data engine leverages the complete memory hierarchy from disk to L1 cache and shifts the curve between big data and fast analysis. And according to Tableau's aggressive product roadmap, the fine-tuning of some of these capabilities as well as several worthwhile new features are on their way. We'll take a closer look at some of the details in a later chapter.

One aspect of Tableau that I find impressive and worthwhile to a larger visual data analytics movement is its focus on building a community of data users and a culture of visual analysis. I encourage you to join the Tableau Community and connect with the resources and peers you will find there.

Installing Tableau Desktop

Tableau Desktop is a fantastic out-of-the-box tool for your visual data analytics needs. While there are many other wonderful visual data analytics tools, software, and languages available, I encourage you to experiment with Tableau as the core technology utilized in this book. There are free trials available for new users, and a wealth of ongoing resources, communities, and other groups to help support your visual analytics journey using Tableau.

If you're new to the software, the following are the current technical specifications needed to install Tableau Desktop:

- **Windows**
  - Microsoft Windows 8/8.1, Windows 10 (x64)
  - 2 GB memory
  - 1.5 GB minimum free disk space
  - CPUs must support SSE4.2 and POPCNT instruction sets

- **Mac**
  - macOS Mojave 10.14, macOS Catalina 10.15, and Big Sur 11.4+
  - Intel processors
  - M1 processors under Rosetta 2 emulation mode
  - 1.5 GB minimum free disk space
  - CPUs must support SSE4.2 and POPCNT instruction sets

How to Use This Text

Like traditional classroom instruction, this book's chapters are organized as individual modules that will be your guide as you learn how to communicate business-relevant implications of visual data analysis using the analytic, visualization, and storytelling capabilities of Tableau. Some chapters provide fundamental learning of core concepts, while others are organized as granular exploration of a single concept.

Although you are not limited to working through this book cover to cover, it is recommended that you do so for incremental development of learning and reinforcement of skills. Each module builds on concepts and skills discussed in the preceding one and may include advancements on working through an end-to-end data project that are necessary before taking the next steps forward.

> **note**
>
> With a very few exceptions, all visualizations and screenshots in this book are created using Tableau 2022 for Mac. Differences in operating system versions are negligible.

Supporting Materials

Beyond the modules of this text, there are several companion materials to support ongoing skills development and learning in fundamental visual analytics. These are intended to go beyond the confines of these chapters and to attempt to keep pace with innovations in Tableau functionality as well as review some of its more nuanced advanced features that are out of scope for this book. These resources are suitable for the workplace, although special attention has been given to classroom use:

- **Website** (www.lindyryanwrites.com/academic): This website acts as an information hub to share all companion materials, including lecture decks, datasets, and more.

- **Pearson Educator Portal:** All non-Tableau-provided sample data, presentation materials, curriculum, and other educator resources are maintained by Pearson Education.

- **Datasets:** All publicly available datasets used in this text are available either from their original source or through www.lindyryanwrites.com. Additionally, Tableau catalogs a wide array of datasets that can be used to practice, teach, or otherwise engage with data visualization.

- **Curricula:** Designed for entry to mid-level analysts, as well as undergraduate and graduate students, selected lecture materials and assignments to support this text are also available. These are hosted and available via Pearson Education for educators. They are incrementally updated and include recommended readings and videos. Guest lecturing services are available to university faculty, as well as corporate training workshops for industry professionals. Tableau also offers educator support with its Tableau for Teaching program, which includes classroom software licensing and curricula kits.

- **Connect with me:** Reach out to me directly on any social media. I love to engage with you and see what stories you are telling with data!
  - **Twitter:** @lindyryanwrites
  - **Tableau Public:** https://public.tableau.com/app/profile/lindy.ryan
  - **LinkedIn:** www.linkedin.com/in/lindyryan/

Contents of This Book

Each chapter in this book pairs fundamental learning with hands-on application of core concepts, and the lessons learned in each chapter are intended to compound as you make your way through the text. Because some aspects require more in-depth discussion while others favor practical application, you may feel some chapters lean one way or another, while others are more equally balanced. You will leave each chapter ready to apply the lesson given, and with an additional layer of knowledge laid over the previous.

The chapters in this book are organized in a pedagogical manner to best support incremental learning. Each is intended to

- Provide a foundation of knowledge that is grounded in best practices and empirical evidence to form the basis for education on the concepts we'll cover.
- Give you the opportunity to get hands on in Tableau and develop working skills to practice core concepts. These chapters provide step-by-step instruction, visual aids, and tips and techniques to expand your software skills.

The following provides a brief overview of what you can expect in each chapter.

Chapter 1: Welcome to Visual Analytics

This chapter introduces the practice of visual analytics with an overview of the state of the data visualization industry. As a foundation for more in-depth explorations throughout this book, we'll explore how data visualization and visual data storytelling have become in-demand analytic job skills today, how the two practices are similar and different, and how both are propelled by new technologies and bigger, more diverse, and more dynamic data. Lastly, we'll examine the role of communication skills within visual analytics and briefly look at how academia is supporting the demand for visual analysts today.

Chapter 2: The Power of Visual Analytics

Memory, retention, and emotion form the understanding for experience, all of which work in tandem with our brains' visual processing horsepower. This chapter leverages real-life examples to showcase the power of visual analytics and visual data stories to communicate discoveries and insights hidden in data. We will review the role of human cognition in visual analytics, how the brain reacts to inputs of data, stories, and data stories as unique entities, and how we can leverage this power to tell impactful data narratives and influence action.

Chapter 3: Getting Started with Tableau

Application requires an environment for practice as a first step toward efficacy. This chapter shifts focus from theory to implementation as we briefly explore the different products contained within the Tableau application suite, focusing on the Tableau Desktop 2022 user interface. We cover how to get started with Tableau Desktop, review the tool's user interface and basic functionality, and discuss how to connect to data and ensure it is properly prepared for analysis. From here, you will be able to move on to the visual analytics process to curate visuals and build data dashboards and stories while building skills and competencies in the market-leading data visualization tool most in demand by today's employers.

Chapter 4: Keeping Visual Analytics in Context

This chapter describes the importance of understanding data's context and its role in helping visual analysts ask the right questions to build a data narrative framework. You'll learn about exploratory and explanatory analysis and strategies for successful data storytelling, including narrative flow, considerations for spoken versus written narratives that support visuals, and structures that can support your stories for maximum impact. We will also explore helpful techniques in Tableau that guide you to crafting effective data narrative structure, and keeping data firmly connected to its context.

Chapter 5: Fundamental Data Visualizations

This chapter introduces the fundamental charts and graphs used to visually communicate data that are offered on the Tableau Show Me Card. We discuss appropriate use cases for each and get hands-on to create examples in Tableau. You will learn techniques to help you assess when to use each visualization type according to the data, how to generate these according to best practices, and helpful considerations for when to avoid certain types of charts. We'll also explore some of the special features available in Tableau to help you get the most from your visual.

Chapter 6: Fundamental Maps

As a continuation of the previous chapter, this chapter introduces two fundamental types of maps available on the Tableau Show Me Card. Again, we'll discuss appropriate use cases for each and get hands-on to create examples in Tableau, as well as how to generate these according to best practices, and helpful considerations specifically for mapping data. We'll also explore some of the special features available in Tableau to help you get the most from your maps.

Chapter 7: Design Tips for Curating Visual Analytics

This chapter dives into human cognition and visual perception to frame how pre-attentive attributes like size, color, shape, and position affect the usability and efficacy of visual analytics. We will explore best practices for how the design elements can be employed to direct an audience's attention and create a visual hierarchy of components to communicate effectively.

Chapter 8: Structuring Analytics for Storytelling: Prep, Dashboards, and Stories

This chapter moves beyond the basics of visual analytics to take our first steps in architecting outputs of analysis in visual data dashboards and stories. We'll begin by taking a closer look at how to prepare data in Tableau, utilizing some messy survey data—a common experience for data storytellers—before building data dashboards and stories that incorporate features like filters, annotations, and highlights to present compelling, meaningful, and actionable outcomes of visual analytics.

Chapter 9: Beyond Fundamentals: Advanced Visualizations

This penultimate chapter explores advanced strategies that go beyond fundamental data visualizations to explore a curated set of advanced data visualizations beyond the Tableau Show Me Card. We'll cover how to create advanced charts that require additional formatting and calculations, including timelines, Likert scale charts, lollipop charts, and more.

Chapter 10: Closing Thoughts

This final chapter recaps the main lessons covered throughout the text. It also serves as a resource kit for life beyond the book by providing checklists of best practices and practical suggestions for continuing to master outputs of visual analytics and discusses additional resources available to support you on this journey.

Appendix

Appendix A, "Tableau Services," provides a list of additional Tableau educational resources.

Let's get started!

Register your copy of *Visual Analytics Fundamentals* on the InformIT site for convenient access to updates and/or corrections as they become available. To start the registration process, go to informit.com/register and log in or create an account. Enter the product ISBN (9780137956821) and click Submit. Look on the Registered Products tab for an Access Bonus Content link next to this product, and follow that link to access any available bonus materials. If you would like to be notified of exclusive offers on new editions and updates, please check the box to receive email from us.

Certain figures in the print edition may not be as distinct as they are in the digital version. To ensure an optimal reading experience, color PDFs of figures are available at https://www.informit.com/store/visual-analytics-fundamentals-creating-compelling-data-9780137956821.

ACKNOWLEDGMENTS

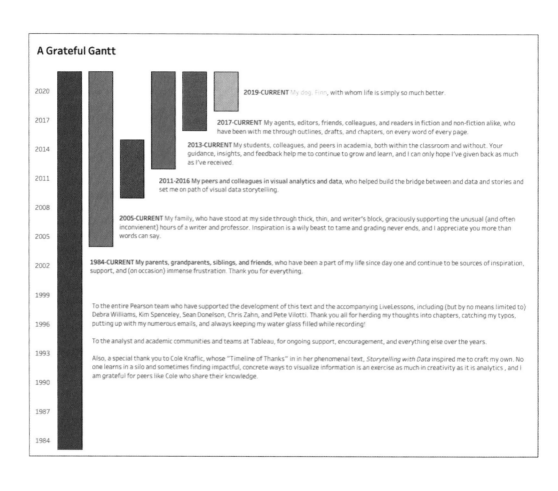

A Grateful Gantt

2019-CURRENT My dog, Finn, with whom life is simply so much better.

2017-CURRENT My agents, editors, friends, colleagues, and readers in fiction and non-fiction alike, who have been with me through outlines, drafts, and chapters, on every word of every page.

2013-CURRENT My students, colleagues, and peers in academia, both within the classroom and without. Your guidance, insights, and feedback help me to continue to grow and learn, and I can only hope I've given back as much as I've received.

2011-2016 My peers and colleagues in visual analytics and data, who helped build the bridge between and data and stories and set me on path of visual data storytelling.

2005-CURRENT My family, who have stood at my side through thick, thin, and writer's block, graciously supporting the unusual (and often inconvienent) hours of a writer and professor. Inspiration is a wily beast to tame and grading never ends, and I appreciate you more than words can say.

1984-CURRENT My parents, grandparents, siblings, and friends, who have been a part of my life since day one and continue to be sources of inspiration, support, and (on occasion) immense frustration. Thank you for everything.

To the entire Pearson team who have supported the development of this text and the accompanying LiveLessons, including (but by no means limited to) Debra Williams, Kim Spenceley, Sean Donelson, Chris Zahn, and Pete Vilotti. Thank you all for herding my thoughts into chapters, catching my typos, putting up with my numerous emails, and always keeping my water glass filled while recording!

To the analyst and academic communities and teams at Tableau, for ongoing support, encouragement, and everything else over the years.

Also, a special thank you to Cole Knaflic, whose "Timeline of Thanks" in in her phenomenal text, *Storytelling with Data* inspired me to craft my own. No one learns in a silo and sometimes finding impactful, concrete ways to visualize information is an exercise as much in creativity as it is analytics , and I am grateful for peers like Cole who share their knowledge.

ABOUT THE AUTHOR

Lindy Ryan is passionate about telling stories with data. She specializes in translating raw data into insightful stories through carefully curated visuals and engaging narrative frameworks.

Prior to joining academia, Lindy worked for The Data Warehousing Institute (TWDI) before becoming the Research Director for research and advisory firm Radiant Advisors from 2011 through 2016. In this role, Lindy led Radiant's analyst activities in the confluence of data discovery and enablement, visualization, and visual analytics. She also developed the Data Visualization Competency Center (DVCC) methodology, a framework for helping data-driven organizations effectively implement data visualization for enterprise-wide visual data analysis and communication. Her tool-agnostic approach has been successfully implemented at a variety of organizations across several industries and with multiple visualization technologies, including Tableau, Qlik, and GoodData, among others.

Lindy began her academic career as an associate faculty member at City University of Seattle's School of Applied Leadership where she taught graduate courses in business leadership from 2013 to 2016. In early 2016, she joined the ambitious team at the Rutgers Discovery Informatics Institute (RDI[2]) and contributed to multidisciplinary research focused on designing solutions for the next generation of supercomputers tasked with enabling cutting-edge extreme-scale science. She also led RDI[2]'s research on understanding and preventing cyberbullying behaviors in emerging technology users through advanced computing approaches and has presented her research at conferences worldwide.

Today, Lindy teaches courses in visual analytics and data visualization in the Professional Science Master's program at Rutgers, the State University of New Jersey. She also formerly taught in the Montclair State University (MSU) Business Analytics program and was the recipient of the MSU Professing Excellence Award, which recognizes professors' teaching excellence, particularly those who inspire and motivate students. She has been a Tableau user since 2012. In addition to her work in analytics, Lindy also serves as guest faculty in Western Connecticut State University's MFA program, mentoring creative writing students working in their second genres.

Lindy is the author of *The Visual Imperative: Creating a Culture of Visual Discovery* (Elsevier Morgan Kaufmann, 2016) and *Visual Data Storytelling with Tableau* (Pearson Addison-Wesley, 2018), as well as numerous papers, book chapters, and conference presentations worldwide. A published novelist, screenwriter, and award-winning short-film director, Lindy's creative work has been adapted for film and has been the recipient of numerous literary awards.

Learn more at www.lindyryanwrites.com.

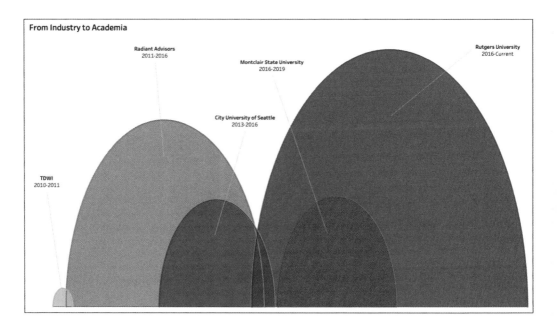

CHAPTER 1

WELCOME TO VISUAL ANALYTICS

This chapter introduces the practice of visual analytics with an overview of the state of the data visualization industry. As a foundation for more in-depth explorations throughout this book, we'll review recent research that highlights how data visualization and visual data storytelling have become in-demand analytic job skills today, how the two practices are similar and different, and how both are propelled by new technologies and bigger, more diverse, and more dynamic data. Lastly, we'll examine the role of communication skills within visual analytics and briefly discuss how industry and academia are supporting the demand for visual analysts today.

A Visual Revolution

In his opening comments at the Tableau User Conference 2022 in Las Vegas, Nevada, Tableau president and CEO Mark Nelson spoke about how the ability to collect, analyze, and understand data at a new scale has created incredible opportunities as well as new challenges, expanding the visual data revolution that has been unfolding across the globe for the better part of the last decade. While using visualization to tell stories about data isn't new (in fact, as you'll soon discover, we've been doing this for quite some time—long before the advent of graphic technology), today we are using visual analytics to share insights about data in more influential and impactful ways than ever before. From academics to politics and everywhere in between, the world's stories are being told through their data points.

Today, the resurgence in the power of data visualization—alongside a virtual gold rush of bigger, more diverse, and more dynamic data—is providing new tools and innovative techniques to help visual analysts transform raw data into compelling visual data narratives through the practices of data visualization and visual data storytelling. Propelled by this newfound horsepower and increasingly self-service visualization technology, we are re-creating the entire analytic process and putting more power in the hands of data analysts. More important, we're making the entire process more visual, radically changing how we explore data to understand and uncover new insights all the way to how we curate dashboards, storyboards, and interactive visualizations so that we can share the fruits of our labor. We are always looking for new ways to show off the messages hidden within our data, and we're getting pretty good at it, too. Information visualizations and rudimentary Excel-based charts and graphs created a decade ago do not compare to the incredible visuals we can now produce with best-of-breed tools like Tableau, or scripting with dynamic JavaScript libraries like D3.js (Figure 1.1).

Our newest breed of data visualizations are moving beyond the classic bar, line, and pie charts of the past, pushing beyond the boundaries of traditional information displays to powerful new territories of graphic representation. With determination and a healthy spirit of curiosity and adventure, visual analysts are visually representing data on everything from static reports to mobile-first delivery platforms and incredible, mural-sized visualizations like the Affinity Map,[1] a 250-square-meter visualization produced by the Swiss Federal Institute of Technology in Lausanne. Likewise, interactive visualizations like Trendalyzer,[2] a statistical animation visualization developed by

---

1. https://actu.epfl.ch/news/the-world-s-largest-data-visualization/
2. www.gapminder.org/tag/trendalyzer/

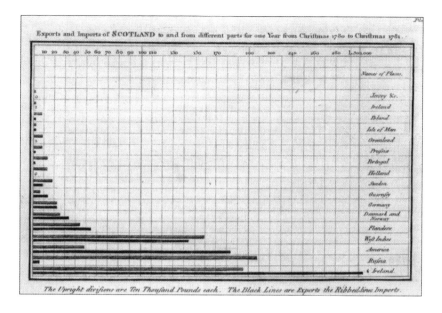

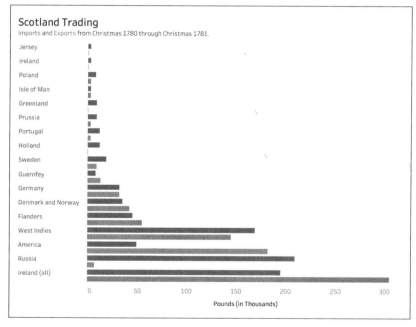

Figure 1.1 An example of "old" data visualization compared to its modern equivalent.

the late Hans Rosling's Gapminder Foundation; streaming visualizations that bring data to life with real-time movement; and fluid, customizable dashboards that toggle between form factors from the desktop to the smartphone with pixel-perfect rendering are giving analysts and audiences alike more capabilities to see and interact with their data. If Gene Roddenberry, creator of the science fiction series *Star Trek*, had scripted today's visual analytics movement, he might have said we are boldly going where no viz has gone before—and he'd be right.

> ## note
>
> Speaking of *Star Trek*, check out how our youngest generation of visual analysts are using the power of data visualization and Tableau to craft engaging new data stories of their own in this "data kids" blog on Tableau: www.tableau.com/blog/viz-long-and-prosper-how-one-young-trekkie-telling-stories-his-data-55767.

However, from the most dynamic to the most static, data visualizations need more than just data to make the leap from information representation to resonation. They need a story—something to show or, more aptly, to "tell" visually—and finding this isn't always obvious when digging through a dataset. It takes exploration, curiosity, and a shift in mindset to move from creating a data visualization to scripting a data narrative. They are similar, but not identical, skill sets. Both require a strong foundation in data analytics and statistics, and both require skills development in the processes of crafting, curating, and sharing data visualizations and stories. And, like any other skill set, ongoing learning—whether at home, through an academic program, or via industry or workplace training—will contribute to continuous enhancement and efficacy in your holistic visual analytics skill set.

Scripting a data narrative might sound like a vague or even overwhelming process. After all, many of us might consider ourselves analysts first—"data people" before storytellers—a sentiment that is echoed by a recent global survey of visual analysts across industries. We may enjoy numbers and analytics and computation more than the craft of curating visuals or crafting stories, and we may also experience frustration when our stakeholders underestimate the amount of time required for other tasks undertaken leading up to visualization (i.e., data prep, analysis, and ideation). Nevertheless, the two are fundamentally intertwined. We must know our data, its context, and the results of analytics if we are to extrapolate these into meaning for an audience who doesn't. That's all a story is, really: one person sharing something new and unknown with another in a way that is easily understandable and relatable. The good news? There's no *one* way to do it. Rather, we can use several proven narrative frameworks to design a data storyboard, and numerous quintessential examples exist where a data storyteller has exercised a generous amount of creative liberty and done something entirely new. Like any kind of story, data stories require a certain amount of creativity, and although tools and technology can do much with our data for us, creativity is a uniquely human contribution to any narrative (Figure 1.2). We'll take a look at more examples as we go forward.

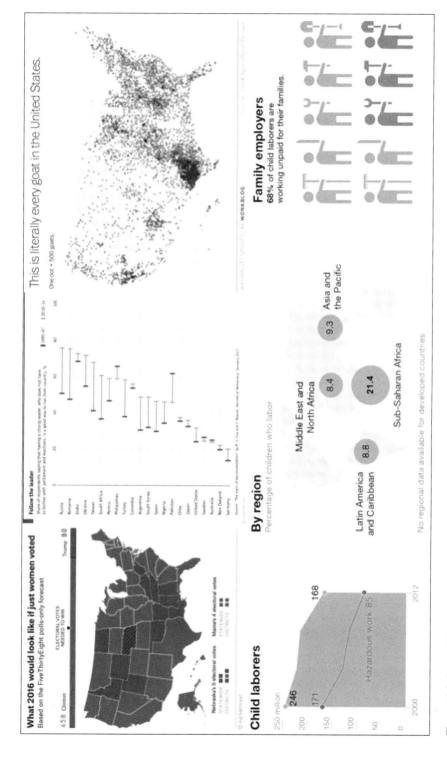

Figure 1.2 A sampling of great data stories in recent headlines by statisticians and data journalists.

> **note**
>
> Data *visualization* is the practice of graphically representing data to help people see and understand patterns, insights, and other discoveries hidden inside information. Data *storytelling* translates seeing into meaning by weaving a narrative around data to answer questions and support decision making.

Data visualization and data storytelling are interrelated concepts within the broader framework of visual analytics, but they are not the same thing. A true data story utilizes data visualizations as a literary endeavor would use illustrations—proof points to support the narrative. However, there's a bit of a role reversal here: Whereas data visualizations provide the "what" in the story, the narrative itself answers the "why." As such, the two work together in tandem to translate raw data into something meaningful for an audience. So, to be a proper data storyteller you need to know how to both curate effective data visualizations *and* frame a storyboard around them. This starts with learning how to properly and effectively visualize data, and how to do so in the best way for presentation rather than for purely analytical purposes. As discussed later in this book, visualizations for analysis versus presentation are not always the same thing.

One of the most commonly encountered phrases in the visual analytics space is "data visualizations are only as effective as the insights they reveal." In this context, effectiveness is a function of careful planning. Any meaningful visualization is a two-pronged one. It requires analytical perfection and correct rendering of statistical information, as well as a well-orchestrated balance of visual design cues (color, shape, size, and so on) to encode that data with meaning. The two are not mutually exclusive.

Data visualization is a place where science meets art, although the jury is still out on whether the practice is more of a scientific endeavor or an artistic one. Although experts agree that a compelling visual requires proper application of both science and art, in practice it tends to be more of a chicken-and-egg scenario. We haven't quite come to a consensus as to whether science comes before design or we design for the science, and the decision changes depending on who you ask, who is creating the visualization, and who the intended audience is. That said, whichever side of the argument you land on, the result is the same: We need statistical understanding of the data, its context, and how to measure it; otherwise, we run the risk of faulty analysis and skewed decision making that eventually lead to more risk and complications. Likewise, our very-visual cognition system demands a way to encode numbers with meaning, so we rely on colors and shapes to help automate these processes for us. Done incorrectly, improper application and encoding of visual information can also lead to faulty analysis, skewed decision making, and risk. An effective visual must strike the right balance of both to accurately and astutely deliver on its goal: intuitive insight at a glance.

This might sound like an easy task, but learning to properly construct correct and effective data visualization isn't something you can accomplish overnight. It takes as much time to master this craft as it does any other, as well as a certain dedication to patience, practice, and keeping abreast of changes in software. In fact, in a recent study, new visual analytics practitioners noted that a top frustration is a lack of technical skill, both in data analytics and in the tools used to accomplish data visualization tasks. Like so many other aspects of data science, data visualization and storytelling tend to evolve over time, so an inherent need exists for continuous learning and adaptation, as well as skills development and continued learning. In a survey that we will explore in detail in a subsequent section, visual analysts expressed a need to dedicate more time to gaining an in-depth understanding of their visualization tools, as well as structured training in design, analysis, statistics, and user experience, among other facets, to improve their visual analytics skills. The lessons in this book are intended to support that need and guide you as you begin your first adventures using visual analytics in Tableau.

The Evolution from Data Visualization to Visual Data Storytelling

With all the current focus on data visualization as the best (and sometimes only) way to see and understand today's biggest and most diverse data, it's easy to think of this practice as a relatively new way of representing data and other statistical information. In reality, the practice of graphing information to visually communicate information stretches back all the way to some of the earliest prehistoric cave drawings where our forebears charted the minutiae of early human life. From there, we turned to visualization through initial mapmaking and continuing through to more modern advances in graphic design and statistical graphics. Along the way, the practice of data visualization has been aided by advancements in both visual design and cognitive science as well as in technology and business intelligence (BI), and these developments have given rise to the advancements that have led to our current state of data analytics.

Likewise, the human tendency to share and pass on knowledge through storytelling is considered the "oldest occupation," and is an innate part of human communication. Indeed, consider how far back we can trace the roots of data visualization—and now consider that storytelling stretches even further into the past. There's even evidence of the cognitive effects of storytelling in our neurology, making it a central way that we learn, remember, and communicate information. This, in turn, has important implications when the goal of a visualization or visual data story is to prepare business decision makers to leave a data presentation with a story in their head that helps them remember your message *and* take action on it. We'll discuss the cognitive and anthropological effects of stories more in later chapters.

Graphing stories is the intersection of data visualization and storytelling. American author Kurt Vonnegut is famously quoted as having said, "There is no reason that the simple shapes of stories can't be fed into a computer—they have beautiful shapes." Likewise, we could restate this to say that data stories provide the shapes to communicate information in ways that facts and figures alone can't. Just as much as today's approach to visual analytics has changed the way we see and understand our data, data storytelling has been the catalyst that has radically changed the way we talk about our data.

Learning to present insights and deliver the results of analysis in visual form involves working with data, employing analytical approaches, choosing the most appropriate visualization techniques, applying visual design principles, and structuring a compelling data narrative. Also, although crafting an effective and compelling visual data story is, like traditional storytelling, a uniquely human experience, tools and software can help. Referring back to Vonnegut's quote, stories have shapes. In visual data storytelling, we find the shape of the story through exploration of the data. The results of analysis (visual or otherwise) help us frame and organize the sequence of the data points, and tools give us the ability to architect visualizations and layer knowledge to tell a story.

To visualize the data storytelling process, consider Figure 1.3. It depicts the visual analytics process we'll follow throughout this book. However, this process isn't always as straightforward or linear as it might initially appear. In reality, this process is, like all discovery processes, iterative. For example, as a result of analysis we might need to revisit data wrangling—we might uncover a missing attribute that we need for our proposed model or need to incorporate supplementary data to complete an insight. Finally, as the story unfolds, we might need to revisit previous steps to support claims we did not originally plan to make.

Figure 1.3 The storytelling process, visualized.

A Brief Look at the State of the Industry

Before we begin learning about visual analytic fundamentals and ways to apply them, let's take a moment to briefly discuss the state of the industry and understand the role of data visualization in the job market today.

Since 2017, the Data Visualization Society (DVS) has fostered a community of visual data analysts whose members benefit from resources that support growth, refinements, and expansion of data visualization knowledge. A growing but specialized group of global data visualization practitioners, DVS members participate in an annual survey—the State of the Industry (SOTI) survey—overseen by the DVS Survey Committee. This survey is intended to "help the DVS and broader data visualization community understand the state of data visualization, the people who make it, the challenges they face, what can help practitioners, and where the field is headed."[3] These findings are often couched in historical context and supported by similar surveys—including Observable's *State of Dataviz* survey and organization Viz for Social Good's community survey.

In 2021, a total of 2,165 respondents from more than 100 different industries and all six populated continents provided usable data for analysis in the DVS SOTI survey, which elicited responses across topics including demographics, roles and tasks, experience and compensation, tools and charts, challenges and changes, COVID-19 impacts, and other forward-looking and role-specific questions. Results are primarily presented descriptively, focusing on group sizes and percentages.

> note
>
> Read the full report, and the corresponding survey data, at www.datavisualizationsociety.org/report-2021.

While the 2021 survey yielded a number of interesting and illuminative findings, perhaps what's most interesting is how inclusive and dynamic the visual analytics playground is. Beyond demographics and representation, which are optimistic and becoming more equitable among underrepresented populations, the survey provides a glimpse into how varied jobs are for visual analysts. Many data visualizers consider themselves analysts, a role that traverses every sector, but corresponding job titles are varied as well—from data scientists to analysts, academics, researchers, graphic designers, data storytellers, journalists, reporters, cartographers, architects, and even biologists, with median annual salaries ranging from USD $80,000 to $99,999.

---

3. www.datavisualizationsociety.org/report-2021

We'll look more closely at the DVS SOTI survey findings in later chapters, and the job market for visual analytics in Chapter 3. However, it's worth noting now that the number of job postings for data visualization–related jobs has increased dramatically over the past decade (Figure 1.4). From fewer than 2,000 jobs in 2010 to more than 100,000 jobs in 2021, the demand for analysts skilled in data visualization has seen tremendous growth, with the future in data viz looking bright indeed. Note that jobs reflected in the data represent the total number of hiring openings posted across the United States that required a minimum of a bachelor's degree.

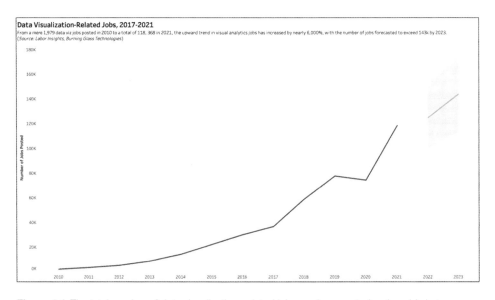

Data Visualization-Related Jobs, 2017-2021
From a mere 1,979 data viz jobs posted in 2010 to a total of 118, 368 in 2021, the upward trend in visual analytics jobs has increased by nearly 6,000%, with the number of jobs forecasted to exceed 143k by 2023. *(Source: Labor Insights, Burning Glass Technologies)*

Figure 1.4 The total number of data visualization–related job openings posted nationwide between 2010 and 2021.

While these studies provide an optimistic glimpse into the future of the visual analytics job market, this upward momentum is not without its challenges, particularly in regard to the amount of training and educational resources to support this tremendous skills need. In early 2022, Tableau tasked Forrester Consulting with researching the role data skills play in business outcomes. The resulting study, titled "Building Data Literacy: The Key to Better Decisions, Greater Productivity, and Data-Driven Organizations," included a survey of more than 2,000 executives, decision makers, and data contributors working at global companies with 500 or more employees in 10 countries. The quick takeaway: Despite the increasing job demand for data skills, there is not yet enough training available.[4]

---

4. www.tableau.com/about/press-releases/2022/new-data-literacy-research

As part of its study, Forrester found that data skills are increasingly crucial—not only as in-demand skills that are seen as most important for today's analysts to succeed in their day-to-day work, but also as the skills that have increased most in importance over the last three years. According to the study, 82% of today's analytic decision makers expect basic data literacy from employees across departments (IT, human resources, and so on). However, while close to 70% of employees are expected to use data heavily in their job by 2025 (a 40% increase from 2018), currently only 39% of organizations make data training available to their employees.

> note
>
> Read the full report at www.tableau.com/sites/default/files/2022-03/ Forrester_Building_Data_Literacy_Tableau_Mar2022.pdf.

From Visual to Story: Bridging the Gap

It's important to recognize that technical competencies are not the only skills in demand by analytic employers today. Data will continue to grow, technologies to adapt and innovate, and analytical approaches to chart new territory to evolve the way we work with and uncover meaning and value hidden within our data. The real value in becoming a data storyteller is to amass the ability to share—to communicate—about our data.

So far, we've put data visualization first and communication second, because that is the order you follow when you structure your visual analysis—you have to explore and build something before you can tell a story about it. However, we shouldn't underestimate the communication that happens before you ever touch your data. Communication skills are a prerequisite listed on every job description, but just how important are these skills in data analysis and visual data storytelling, and why?

In 2012, academic researchers with the AIS Special Interest Group on Decision Support, Knowledge, and Data Management Systems (SIG DSS) and Teradata University Network (TUN) formed the Business Intelligence Congress 3 to survey and assess the state of BI and analytics across industries. They surveyed more than 400 recruiters from technical companies, asking which skills and competencies they looked for in new analytic hires. Their number one answer: at more than 58%, communication skills.[5]

---

5. Wixom, Barbara; Ariyachandra, Thilini; Douglas, David; Goul, Michael; Gupta, Babita; Iyer, Lakshmi; Kulkarni, Uday; Mooney, John G.; Phillips-Wren, Gloria; and Turetken, Ozgur. "The Current State of Business Intelligence in Academia: The Arrival of Big Data," *Communications of the Association for Information Systems* 34 (2014): Article 1.

The BI Congress survey isn't the only piece of data, or the most recent, to point out the importance of communication skills in analytics. A recent study from data research and advisory firm Gartner sought to determine why big data projects fail—that is, what percentage of big data projects fail due to organizational problems, such as communication, versus what percentage fail due to technical problems, such as programming or hardware.[6] Only about 1% of companies responded that technical issues alone were the fail point of their data analytics problems. The other 99% of companies said that at least half of the reason their data analytics projects failed was due to poor organizational skills—specifically, communication—and not technical skills.

Perhaps most conclusively, we can look directly to the job market to snapshot which communication skills are most in demand by today's employers specifically hiring analysts skilled in visual analytics and data visualization. These top communication skills are depicted in Figure 1.5 and include, in order, teamwork/collaboration, research, written communication, problem-solving, planning, detail-oriented, creativity, and organizational skills. We will look further at technical and software skills prized by today's analytic employers in Chapter 3.

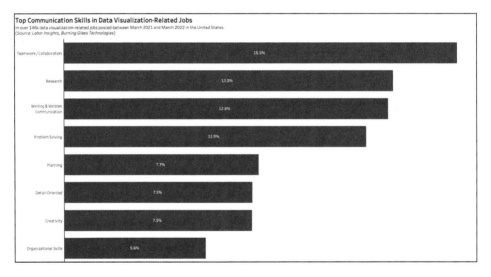

Figure 1.5 In more than 146,000 data visualization–related jobs posted between March 2021 and March 2022 in the United States, these communication skills ranked among the most in demand by today's analytics employers.

---

6. www.gartner.com/newsroom/id/2593815

Of course, there isn't a perfect correlation between organizational skills and communication, but the reality is that one of the most important organizational skills *is* the ability to communicate—hence its inclusion in every business academic program and in every aforementioned job posting. Although communication skills might live on the softer side of things in terms of skill sets, they are nonetheless critical for success, particularly when helping others to see the story within data. If we can't communicate, we can't inspire change or action. Real communication is a two-way dialogue between a sender and one or more receivers. It prompts an action, supports a decision, or generates understanding.

When we discuss the importance of communication skills within the context of data storytelling, we are looking at it from an audience-first perspective. This means putting the audience's needs ahead of the storytellers'. Successful communication hinges on the ability to influence the people who matter the most—the stakeholder for your analysis, be that an executive, a teacher, the general public, or anyone else. Ultimately, how data, visual or otherwise, is interpreted is fundamentally influenced by context. Context is a multifaceted thing. It is driven in part by your audience, but just as important to your story is the part of the context driven by you—your assumptions, your goals, and what you already know.

Understanding the importance of context in analytics is the focus of Chapter 4. For now, we will answer the question posed earlier, "How important are communication skills in visual data storytelling?" with just one word: paramount.

A NOTE ABOUT "DESSERT CHARTS"

After more than two centuries of use (the first being credited to William Playfair's *Statistical Breviary* of 1801), what have come to be called "dessert charts"—circular visualizations including pie and doughnut charts that "slice" data into wedges reminiscent of our favorite sweets—have had a bit of a fall from grace. Although they are still widely in use, many visualization experts and educators preach against the use of these types of charts. However, it should be noted that hatred of pie charts is not merely an opinion, and empirical research provides the rationale for why these types of charts just don't work analytically. That said, there are ways to use them productively, particularly as mechanisms for data storytelling, if a few words of caution are followed. We'll take a deeper look at how to best curate "dessert charts"—and new innovations for crafting useful circular visualizations—in later chapters.

DATA SCIENCE EDUCATION GETS ON THE MAP

By now we are all in agreement: The business of data is changing. Business users are more empowered to work with data; IT is shifting its focus to be less about control and more about enablement. New analytics job descriptions—for example, data scientist and visual data artist—are springing up as companies look for the right people with the right skill sets to squeeze more value from their data. Data itself is getting bigger, hardware more economical, and analytical software more "self-sufficient." We've embraced the paradigm shift from traditional BI to iterative data discovery, and we're becoming increasingly visual, depending on data visualization and storytelling to see, understand, and share data in ways like never before. It's the visual imperative in action.

As you might expect, these changes have a significant effect on how people work across analytics functions, be they executives and leadership, data scientists, analysts, or even data storytellers. There are a lot of skills available and a very big toolbox to choose tools from, and we are all learning together. Adding to that, over the past few years we've been reminded that data workers are in high demand, and we've seen firsthand how limited the current supply is. This means we have to start thinking about cultivating talent rather than recruiting it, and training an incoming workforce isn't something that an industry can do alone, no matter how many specialized software training programs, massive open online courses (MOOCs), conferences, and excellent publications we produce. In fact, one finding uncovered in the 2021 DVS SOTI survey was a lack of structured programs and stronger foundational knowledge bases, which respondents said are needed to nurture visual analytic skills development for both new and established analysts. According to the survey, data visualizers are continuously looking to learn new skills, with 26.8% prioritizing new skills, 24.3% wanting to improve skills with an existing tool, and 25.9% interested in learning a new tool.

To enact lasting change and ensure a sustainable funnel of competent data workers suited to the new era of the data industry, we need to move further down the pipeline to that place where we all discovered we wanted to be data people in the first place: the classroom. And that's exactly what the academic community is doing. Tasked with developing new courses and degree programs that develop the skills and provide foundational education needed by analytics professionals, university information science programs focusing on business analytics and data science for the business community are growing exponentially across the country—and enrollment is promising.

Different universities are taking different approaches to structuring a new kind of analytics education. Some are developing entirely new pedagogy focused on the fluid and dynamic fields of data science. Others are reshaping existing curricula by unifying across academic silos to integrate disciplines of study, particularly among the business and IT domains. Others are forming academic alliance programs to give students learning experiences with contemporary industry tools and creating projects that expose students to analytical problems within real-world business contexts.

All universities are listening to campus recruiters and market research that demonstrate the need for qualified, educated people with more data skills and knowledge, and they're working hard to fill that gap. The top programs are focused on real-world applications of data problems and are doing their best to keep pace with fluid changes in technology adoption, new programming languages, and on-the-market software packages. They're also putting a premium on visual analytics. Vendors like Tableau, with its Tableau for Teaching program, are helping, too.

So just how big is data science education? Over the past couple of years, the number of new business analytics program offerings has significantly increased. In 2010, there were a total of 131 confirmed, full-time BI/BA university degree programs, including 47 undergraduate-level programs. By 2018, that number had tripled. As of this writing, there are now at least 69 undergraduate programs, 438 masters programs, 24 doctorate programs, and more than 100 certificates available at U.S.-based academic institutions (Figure 1.6). So, while we might not have access to all this new data talent yet, if academia has anything to say about it, help is on the way.

note

This dataset is regularly updated and maintained by Ryan Swanstrom and is available via Github at https://github.com/ryanswanstrom/awesome-datascience-colleges.

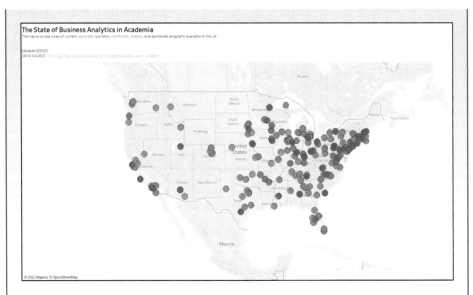

The State of Business Analytics in Academia
The map provides a key of current associate, bachelor, certificate, master, and doctorate programs available in the US.

Updated 8/2022
DATA SOURCE:

© 2022 Mapbox © OpenStreetMap

Figure 1.6 Business analytics degree programs in the United States.

Summary

This chapter provided an introductory discussion of the practice of visual analytics and an overview of the state of the data visualization industry, while giving special consideration to the exponential growth in employment and academic programs to support technical and other skills development in new and emerging visual analysts. The next chapter takes a closer look at human cognition and the power of visualization to help us understand what makes visual communication so powerful and important in today's data deluge before we begin going hands on to apply learning directly in Tableau.

CHAPTER 2

THE POWER OF VISUAL ANALYTICS

Memory, retention, and emotion form the understanding for experience, all of which work in tandem with our brains' visual processing horsepower. This chapter leverages real-life examples to showcase the power of visual analytics and visual data stories to communicate discoveries and insights hidden in data. We will review the role of human cognition in visual analytics; consider how the brain reacts to inputs of data, stories, and data stories as unique entities; and explore how we can leverage this power to tell impactful data narratives and influence action.

The Science of Storytelling

The world of data is changing. So is how we tell stories about it.

In a September 2016 interview with NPR Marketplace,[1] *National Geographic*'s then editor-in-chief Susan Goldberg spoke to host Kai Ryssdal about the power of visual storytelling, which has provided a transformative conduit for the publication in the new digital era. Speaking about the media company's long history of photojournalism and its recent digital conversion from traditional print magazine to social media heavy-weight, Goldberg commented that "everything is visual today"—especially stories. It's worth noting that *National Geographic* is dominating visual storytelling online, using powerful imagery to captivate and educate (as of this writing) 60.5 million Instagram followers, 28 million Twitter followers, and 49 million Facebook followers, in addition to its Snapchat and TikTok channels (the latter currently totaling 2 million followers). The magazine is also throwing its hat into the ring with data visualization through its Data Points blog. In fact, *National Geographic* is something of a gold standard for print companies going digital: Time Inc. CEO Joe Ripp used *National Geographic* as a guide for turning *Time* into a "digital powerhouse"[2]—and part of that blueprint is the success *National Geographic* has had in social media.

Media and journalists aren't the only ones putting an emphasis on data storytelling, although they have certainly been a particularly imaginative bunch of communica-tors. Today we've seen the power of storytelling used to color in conversations on just about every type of data imaginable—from challenging astronomical principles to visualizing the tenure pipeline at Harvard Business School to quantifying the fairytale of Little Red Riding Hood. Speaking of social media, it's clear how visual interfaces like Instagram, Snapchat, and TikTok have reshaped digital content and engagement. A new app, Lucid, even uses the power of visualization as its core differentiator from its main competitor, Twitter, by noting in its mission statement, "By visualizing and clarifying complex insights from the world's greatest thinkers, we're helping people around the world master essential topics and learn new skills, quickly and easily."[3] In every organization and every industry, visual data stories are becoming the next script for how we share information, and we are harnessing the power of visual analytics to tell them.

---

1. www.marketplace.org/2016/09/26/sustainability/corner-office-marketplace/
   dont-call-national-geographic-stodgy
2. www.vox.com/2014/9/4/11630542/time-inc-to-take-page-from-national-geographic-playbook
3. https://lucid.fyi/about/

But as diverse as data stories can be, they all have one thing in common: They give us something to connect to in a very literal sense. Now that we have a firm grasp of the market for visual analytics skills, let's delve into the power of stories, first by looking behind the curtain at the science of storytelling and then by examining some incredible existing data stories to see how they have capitalized on the secret sauce of visual analytics.

The Brain on Stories

Chapter 1 mentioned that evidence exists of the cognitive effects of storytelling embedded within our neurology. Here's how: When we are presented with data, only two parts of our brain respond. Both perform functions related to language processing: Wernicke's area is responsible for language comprehension, and Broca's area is responsible for language production. For the very powerful human brain, processing data is easy. The brain's response to these stimuli is a relatively simple input-and-respond transaction that requires the utilization of these two basic areas. Because we're focused only on seeing and responding to information (agree/disagree), there's no great need to overexert our neuro-horsepower.

Unlike simple data, stories—of any kind—require a substantial cognitive boost. Here's an easy thought exercise. Imagine that pasta is on the menu for dinner tonight. However, our pantry is empty, so to prepare this meal we need to go to the grocery store and pick up some supplies. Let's make a quick mental list of our ingredients: pasta noodles, pasta sauce, perhaps herbs, garlic, and Parmesan cheese. If we're feeling fancy, we can grab a loaf of garlic bread or perhaps a bottle of wine as well. You may have just "seen" each of these items flash through your mind as we've listed them—perhaps the familiar size and/or shape of each ingredient, or a favorite brand or logo.

Moving forward, let's pretend we get to the store, only to discover it's closed. So, instead of cooking, we decide to go to our favorite Italian restaurant for our pasta fix. Suddenly the image changes: We're no longer visualizing individual items on a grocery list but turning toward imagining an immersive visual experience—a waiter setting down a big, beautiful dish of steaming, flavorful, scent-rich spaghetti. Perhaps we also hear the buzzing backdrop of restaurant sounds—low-volume music, water glasses being filled, the clink of silverware, and so on. If we think about it long enough (or if we're hungry enough), we can almost *taste* the food.

Now, imagine your favorite dish served at a holiday feast and pay attention to what other senses engage. These might include memories and other auditory information more personally meaningful than a typical restaurant experience.

This is the difference between visualizing data and presenting a story: Rather than itemizing a list of ingredients (data points), we are presenting a full, sensory-engaging dining experience (Figure 2.1).

Figure 2.1 Visualizing versus presenting.

A more traditional way of thinking about this storytelling experience is to consider the difference between reading a novel and watching a film. When reading, you are tasked with using your imagination; you're reading the raw data of words and building the story in your mind. Conversely, when you watch a film, your imagination is off the hook. Images of characters and settings, costumes, spoken dialogue, music, and so on are designed and displayed for you on the screen to ingest, rather than generate. When you watch a live presentation, such as a stage play or a 4D movie, you may also get a few extra pieces of sensory information, like the smell of a smoke machine or carefully chosen scents pumping through the air to accompany the story.

These extra storytelling details have a profound effect on the brain (Figure 2.2). Beyond the two areas of the brain that become activated when presented with data, five additional areas respond when presented with a story:

- The visual cortex (colors and shapes)
- The olfactory cortex (scents)
- The auditory cortex (sounds)
- The motor cortex (movement)
- The sensory cortex/cerebellum (language comprehension)

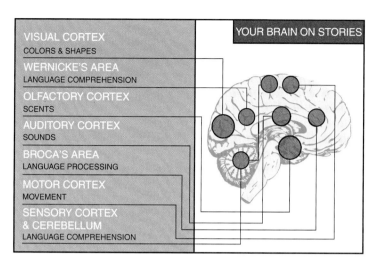

Figure 2.2 The brain on stories.

The Human on Stories

Beyond the cognitive sciences, there's a lot of anthropological truth to the old adage, "Everyone loves a good story."

Storytelling has been an integral part of human expression and culture throughout time. All human cultures tell stories, and most people derive a great deal of pleasure from them, even if they are untrue (think of fantastical stories or fables). Beyond pure entertainment value (which, frankly, is not to be disregarded), stories teach us important lessons. We learn from them. In many cases, they are how we transmit information—whether through metaphoric tales, instructions, or legends. Stories also have the ability to transport us; we give the author license to stretch the truth—although, in data storytelling, this license extends only as far as it can before the data loses its elasticity and begins to break down. Data stories, above all, must be true. They are works of narration, but definitively nonfiction (sometimes called "data documentaries").

Okay, so we love stories—but why? There's no easy answer to this question, and from academe to industry, the research is crowded with books and articles attempting to explain the cognitive and anthropological basis of human storytelling and literature under the heading of storytelling psychology. It's a *lot* to think about (and, of course, a lot to read!). However, for the purposes of this book, we can distill these dialogues into two primary possible contenders for *why* we tell stories: the need to survive (fitness) and the need to know (closure).

Fitness

As much as we might try to argue otherwise, human beings simply did not evolve to find truth. Rather, we evolved to defend positions and obtain resources—often regardless of the physical or mental cost—so that we could survive. These concepts lie at the heart of Darwinian theory of natural selection: *survival* of the fittest as the mechanism, and our ability to overcome (or, biologically, to reproduce), known as *fitness*.

Human biology aside, to survive in competitive and often unstable environments, whether wilderness or business, one thing we've always had to do is understand other people. In fact, one of our most expensive cognitive tasks, where we exert an impressive amount of energy, is in trying to figure out other people—predict what they're going to do, understand motivations, assess relationships, and so forth. Beyond people, we are driven to understand how things work. If we know how they work, we can conquer, fix, or control them. All of these lead to "winning," which equates to survival and continuation. Stories act as guides that give us the information and confidence we need to harness this knowledge—sort of instruction manuals for things we encounter throughout life. By doing so, they increase our fitness.

Closure

Aside from being bent on survival, humans tend to require closure. A few philosophical exceptions notwithstanding, in general we don't enjoy ongoing questions and curiosities with no resolution. We *need* endings, even unhappy ones. We simply can't abide cliffhangers; they're sticky in the worst of ways, bouncing around in our brains until we can finally "finish" them and put them to rest (just read any book review website to see this in action). There's actually a term for this phenomenon—the *Zeigarnik effect*, named for Soviet psychologist Bluma Zeigarnik. Zeigarnik demonstrated that people have a better memory for unfinished tasks than they do for finished ones. Today, the Zeigarnik effect is known formally as a psychological device that creates dissonance and uneasiness in the target audience.

In essence, the Zeigarnik effect speaks to our human need for endings. No matter the story's goal—to focus, align, teach, or inspire—we build narratives to foster imagination, excitement, and even speculation. Successful narratives are those that grab the audience's attention, work through a message, and then resolve our anxiety with a satisfactory ending. Thus, stories are therapeutic. They give us closure.

The Power of Stories

We've established that data stories are powerful, and that they are powerful because of their ability to communicate information, generate understanding and knowledge, and stick in our brains over the long term. However, as information assets, visual data stories have a few other noteworthy qualities.

But first, let's set the record straight. There is much to be said about how visual data stories create meaning in a time of digital data deluge, but it would be careless to relegate data storytelling to the role of "a fun new way to talk about data." Visual data storytelling has *radically changed* the way we talk about data (though certainly not invented the concept). The traditional charts and graphs we've long used to represent data are still helpful because they help us to better visually organize and understand information and because they are cemented as one of the ways in which we visually organize and understand data. They've just become a little static.

With today's technology, fueled by today's innovation, we've moved beyond the mentality of gathering, analyzing, and reporting data to collecting, exploring, and sharing information. Instead of simply rendering data visually, we are now focused on using these mechanisms to engage, communicate, inspire, and make data memorable. No longer resigned to the tasks of beautifying reports or dashboards, data visualizations are lifting out of paper, coming out of the screen, and moving into our hearts, minds, and emotions. In fact, the ability to stir emotion is the secret ingredient of visual data storytelling, and what sets it apart from the aforementioned static information visualization renderings.

As we'll explore in later chapters, emotional appeal isn't enough to complete a meaningful visual data story. Like any good tale, a data story requires an anchor or a goal, be it a reveal, a call to action, or an underlying message to pass on to its audience. This idea isn't unique to visual data storytelling by any means, but a construct applied to all varieties of stories—and to all varieties of analytics. When a story imprints on our memory, it requires emotion plus a willingness to act on that emotion.

Instead of talking about the power of visual data stories, let's see them in action within the context of visual analytics. As we do, we'll be looking for the following key takeaways:

- Sometimes the only way to see the story in data is visually.
- A good story should meet its goals, and it should be actionable.
- A story should change, challenge, or confirm the way you think.
- Storytelling evolves—don't be afraid to try something new.

The Classic Visualization Example

One of the core tenets of a visual data story is that it uses different forms of data analytics and visualization (e.g., charts, graphs, infographics) to bring data to life. Perhaps one of the most archetypal examples of the power of visual analytics to help people see and understand data in ways they never would by looking at a simple data table—rows and columns of raw black and white data—comes from Anscombe's Quartet (Figure 2.3).

I		II		III		IV	
X	Y	X	Y	X	Y	X	Y
10	8.04	10	9.14	10	7.46	8	6.58
8	6.95	8	8.14	8	6.77	8	5.76
13	7.58	13	8.74	13	12.74	8	7.71
9	8.81	9	8.77	9	7.11	8	8.84
11	8.33	11	9.26	11	7.81	8	8.47
14	9.96	14	8.1	14	8.84	8	7.04
6	7.24	6	6.13	6	6.08	8	5.25
4	4.26	4	3.1	4	5.38	10	12.5
12	10.84	12	9.13	12	8.15	8	5.56
7	4.82	7	7.26	7	6.42	8	7.91
5	5.68	5	4.74	5	5.73	8	6.88
MEAN	9.00	7.5	9.00	7.5	9.00	7.5	9.00	7.5
STD	3.32	2.03	3.32	2.03	3.32	2.03	3.32	2.03
CORR	0.82		0.82		0.82		0.82	
LIN REG	y = 3.00 + 0.500x		y = 3.00 + 0.500x		y = 3.00 + 0.500x		y = 3.00 + 0.500x	

Figure 2.3 Four seemingly identical datasets known as Anscombe's Quartet.

> note
>
> A data table is not considered a data visualization.

Constructed in 1973 by statistician Francis Anscombe, these four datasets appear identical when compared by their summary statistics. If you review the table, you will notice that each dataset has the same mean for both X and Y, the same standard deviation, the same correlation, and the same linear regression equation.

Even though the individual variables are different, if the statistical outputs are the same, we would expect these datasets, when graphed, to *look* the same. The "story" for each of these datasets should be the same—right? Wrong.

Graphing these datasets (Figure 2.4) allows us to see beyond the limitations of basic statistical properties for describing data. We can then appreciate the bigger picture presented by the datasets and the relationships within them.

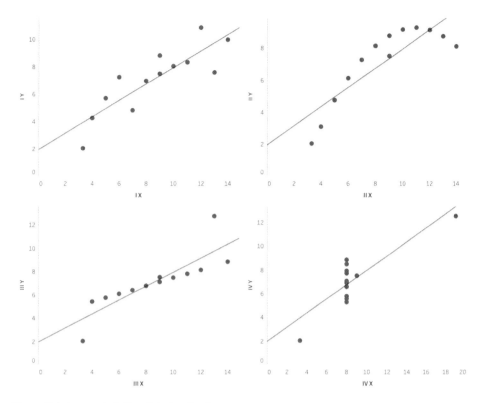

Figure 2.4 Anscombe's Quartet, visualized.

Anscombe's example might be a classic in terms of putting some support behind visual horsepower, but it only brushes the tip of the iceberg in terms of visual data storytelling. Although we might not yet have everything we need to tell a story, we can start to see that the datasets are not so similar as they might appear, and there is *something* worth talking about in these datasets. We know there is a story there, and we know we need to visualize it to see it, but we are still left wanting. This isn't quite a visual data story, but it's definitely a first step.

Story Takeaway

Sometimes the only way to see the story in data is visually.

Using Small Personal Data for Big Stories

When it comes to telling a story, no one knows how to do it better than Hollywood— except maybe streaming networks like Netflix (always the disrupter), Amazon Prime, and AMC, which are using massive amounts of consumer-generated data as recipes to create new content.

Graphic designer Chelsea Carlson decided to take this approach to a personal level. In a 2016 experiment, Chelsea focused on analyzing her personal Netflix viewing habits to see what story her own data might tell about her television bingeing habits, tastes, and preferences. Perhaps more important in a streaming TV market saturated with more new shows every day, that story might even help her predict a new favorite by telling her exactly what to look for. (This approach is not too radical a departure from how Netflix et al. leverage user-viewing data to curate new shows.)

Like many analysts, Chelsea began her experiment by collecting and organizing her Netflix viewing data in spreadsheets organized in Excel. She tracked several variables on her top 27 favorite shows, including things like genre, language, main character's gender, episode length, IMDB rating, and more (Figure 2.5). As a tool, a color-coded spreadsheet helped Chelsea get a bird's-eye view of some of the interesting patterns and trends in her data (e.g., whether she seemed to prefer multi-season shows or whether her favorites aligned with award winners) as well as areas where her tastes were less predictable (no preference for age and race of the lead character or the show's setting or length). However, this was the extent of meaningful analysis that Chelsea could achieve when limited to scouring rows and columns of information— even colored ones (see the sidebar "Color Cues").

show name	time period	main character	length	costume drama	# of seasons	years on the	IMDB us	IMDB # of users	golden	show creator
d Men	mid 20th	man	45	yes	7	2007-2015	8.7	131,187	4	Mathew Weiner
vet	mid 20th	ensemble	60	yes		2013-	7.9	879	0	Ramón Campos, Gema R. ?
andal	present	woman	45	yes	4+	2012-	7.9	45,209	0	Shonda Rhimes
REAL	present	woman	45	no	5+	2015-	7.8	3,732	0	Marti Noxon, Sarah Gert...
e Office	present	ensemble	20	no	9	2005-2013	8.8	179,606	1	Greg Daniels, Ricky Gerv...
rks & Recreation	present	woman	20	no	7	2009-2015	8.6	103,152	1	Greg Daniels, Michael Sc...
wnton Abbey	early 20th	ensemble	60	yes	6	2010-2015	8.7	98,003	3	Julian Fellowes
erlock	present	man	45	no	4+	2010-	9.3	430,133	0	Mark Gatiss, Steven Mof...
pire	present	ensemble	45	yes	2+	2015-	8	20,544	0	Lee Daniels, Danny Stro...
fly	future (2517)	man	45	yes	1	2002-2003	9.1	171,351	0	Joss Whedon
ested Development	present	man	20	no	5	2003-2013	9	195,532	1	Mitchell Hurwitz
tes Motel	retro present	woman	45	yes	3+	2013-	8.1	49,820	0	Anthony Cipriano, Carlto...
aks & Geeks	1980s	woman	45	no	1	1999-2000	8.9	82,813	1	Paul Feig
ilight Zone	assorted	ensemble	20	no	5	1959-1964	9	39,253	1	Rod Serling
ad City	present	woman	20	no	3+	2014-	8.5	10,154	0	Ilana Glazer, Abbi Jacobs...
shing Daisies	retro present	couple	45	yes	2	2007-2009	8.4	42,479	0	Bryan Fuller
-So-Called Life	present	woman	45	no	1	1994-1995	8.4	14,541	1	Winnie Holzman
nge is the New Black	present	women ensemb	45	no	4	2013-	8.4	159,370	0	Jenji Kohan
erican Horror Story	assorted	ensemble	45	yes	5	2011-	8.3	173,899	1	Brad Falchuk, Ryan Murp...
ad Like Me	present	woman	45	no	2	2003-2004	8.2	33,669	0	Bryan Fuller
a Riches	present	couple	45	no	1.5	2007-2008	8	7,004	0	Dmitry Lipkin
e Tudors	17th century	man	45	yes	4	2007-2010	8.1	47,512	0	Michael Hirst
fy the Vampire Slayer	present	woman	45	no	7	1997-2003	8.2	96,018	0	Joss Whedon
llhouse	present	woman	45	no	2	2009-2010	7.8	38,314	0	Joss Whedon
ject Runway	present	ensemble	45	yes	14+	2004-	7.3	7,881	2	n/a
a Grand Hotel	early 20th	ensemble	60	yes	3	2011-2013	8.5	2,079	0	n/a

Figure 2.5 Chelsea Carson's Netflix data spreadsheet, in table form.

As with Anscombe's Quartet, when Chelsea plotted her data, the visualization transformed the data beyond its meager Excel boundaries and moved it into the realm of storytelling. Now Chelsea was telling a much richer tale via visual analytics (Figure 2.6).

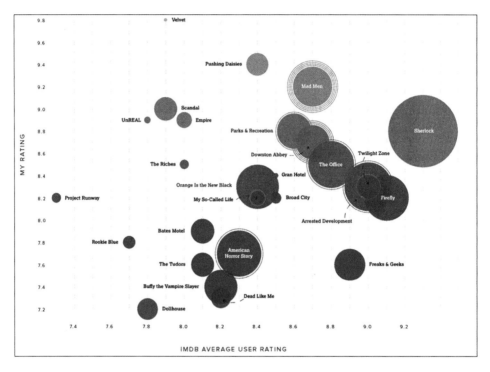

Figure 2.6 Chelsea Carlson's Netflix data visualized.

As a visual storyteller, Chelsea worked through visual discovery and analytics processes and designed a variety of graph types that included scatter plots, packed bubble charts, timelines, and even pie charts to build her data story. She also integrated expressive visual elements, particularly size and color, to provide visual cues to assign meaning to the visualization and highlight certain insights (we'll discuss these building blocks of visualization later). As a result, Chelsea was able to come away with a rich visual data story encapsulated within a series of very deliberately crafted visualizations. There are several interesting story points to pick out within this visualization—including a strong bias for costume dramas and shows cut short (something that would be interesting to investigate in an updated analysis, with Netflix shows like *Bridgerton* now in the mix). However, perhaps the most salient point is that through her visual analytics work, Chelsea developed a visual data story that can help her take action on the goals she set for this analysis project. She can clearly see her tastes and preferences, and when she goes scrolling through Netflix for her next binge-worthy show, she'll know to look for a female-led costume drama with a genre-bending storyline.

Story Takeaway

A good story should meet its goals, and it should be actionable.

COLOR CUES

The Netflix experiment brings to mind an important learning point about the power of data visualization. One of the most important lessons in visual analytics is learning how to leverage *pre-attentive features*—a limited set of visual properties that are detected very rapidly (approximately 200 to 250 milliseconds) and accurately by our visual system and are not constrained by display size. A good visualization—the building blocks of a visual data story—reduces time to insight and leverages our brain's pre-attentive features to keep this time as low as possible.

Let's take a look at the pre-attentive feature known as *perceptual pop-out*—the use of color as a beacon to pre-attentively detect items of importance within the visualization. The shape, size, or color of the item here is less important than its ability to "pop out" of a display. Further, these pop-outs should be used sparingly, and with intention. Presenting too many of these features at once dulls their impact or, worse, can have a detrimental effect on your visualization.

Consider a visit to the eye doctor, when your vision is tested by the ability to spot a flash of color in a sea of darkness. As another example, take a look at Figure 2.7.

	2013	2014	2015	2016
Target	22.27B	21.44B	21.34B	21.79B
Disney	9.45B	22.39B	24.1B	25.64B
Starbucks	8.51B	9.59B	11.38B	12.8B

Figure 2.7 A table showing companies with respective annual gross profits, 2013–2016. Note: All data gathered from www.amigobulls.com.

This is a simple data table with only three companies. Now suppose I asked you to tell me, in each year, which company had the highest gross profit. You are tasked with analyzing each box of the table, line by line, to assess each year independently and select the highest number. You might even have to write it down or mark it in some way to help you remember the winner. Go ahead and give it a try. It should take you roughly one minute to complete the exercise.

Now, take a look at Figure 2.8 and try again.

	2013	2014	2015	2016
Target				
Disney				
Starbucks				

Figure 2.8 A highlight table showing companies with respective annual gross profits, replaced by color, 2013–2016.

Note: All data gathered from www.amigobulls.com.

This time, we've replaced the numerical data with a visual cue—and, coincidentally transformed this representation from a data table to a data visualization type called a highlight table. The simple power of this visualization is that, rather than reading the table, the perceptual pop-out of this design makes completing this exercise a near-instant feat. We don't have to actually "look" for answers; we simply "see" them instead.

Because the sample we are looking at is so small, this is a good time to remark on the special partnership between color and counting. Essentially, the fewer things there are to count, the more quickly we can count them. Makes sense, right? If I were to ask you which company outperformed the others, Disney would be an easy response— it has three out of four of the orange squares.

Our ability to "count" visually is called *numerosity*. This numerical intuition pattern allows us to see an amount without actually counting it. Interestingly, this ability varies among individuals, although the typical counting amount ranges between two and ten items.

As you build visualizations as part of your storyboard framework, be sure to pay careful attention to color and counting to help your audience easily and intuitively experience your story. We'll take a closer look at color and other visual design elements in a later chapter.

The Two-or-Four Season Debate

In school, we're taught that a full year includes four distinct seasons: spring, summer, fall, and winter. Yet, some people argue that only two true seasons exist—summer and winter—and they're using a form of visual data storytelling (and a good heaping of rationality) to prove their point. My favorite of these approaches comes from artificial intelligence researcher Nate Soares's blog, Minding Our Way.[4]

---

4. http://mindingourway.com/there-are-only-two-seasons/

The item up for debate in this story is a simple one: Is it fair to qualify "waxing summer" (also known as spring) and "waning summer" (also known as autumn) as full seasons? Sure, it's *familiar*, and if you live in the northern hemisphere you can likely distinguish the seasons according to their observable natural phenomena, such as their colorful transitions (flowers blooming or leaves changing color) or other sensory ones (weather temperatures) rather than their actual astronomical dates—and this doesn't even begin to open the conversation on astronomical versus meteorological dates of change.[5]

Let's begin to build a story around this question and see where we end up. First, let's agree on a foundation: The year follows a seasonal cycle that starts cold and gets progressively warmer until it peaks and begins to cool again. Repeat. This is a pretty basic assumption. More important, it's one that we can successfully chart loosely and without requiring any more specific data or numbers. Rather, we'll use points from the basic story premise we laid out earlier to graph a seasonal continuum for the year, using length of daylight as our curve (Figure 2.9). From there, we can try to decide just how many seasons are really in a year.

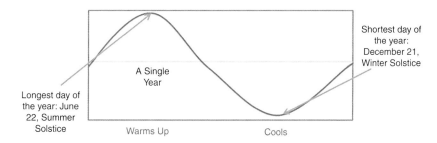

Figure 2.9 The seasonal cycle of a single year.

How many curves does the orange line trace? The answer, obviously, is two—hence the two-season viewpoint (Figure 2.10).

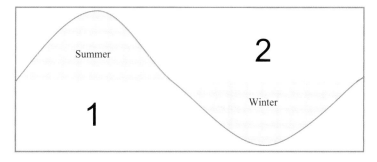

Figure 2.10 Two seasons.

5. www.ncdc.noaa.gov/news/meteorological-versus-astronomical-seasons

From here, we could break this down further with more information. For example, we could add in astronomical dates or mull over geographic differences in weather or meteorology using maps and topography. However, whether you agree with Nate and me (and others!) on the number of qualifying seasons that occur over the course of one year, the preceding two graphs represent a powerful data story without requiring the type of "hard data" (rows and columns of numbers) that we would typically expect. They show us, quite literally, that to tell a great story doesn't necessarily require a ton of data—or much at all. It just requires a few points, a goal, and the creativity to visualize it for your audience in a way that affects their opinion.

Story Takeaway

A story should change, challenge, or confirm the way you think.

Napoleon's March

As I've mentioned, using visualizations to tell stories about data is not a new technique. French civil engineer Charles Joseph Minard has been credited for several significant contributions in the field of information graphics, among them his very unique visualizations of two military campaigns: Hannibal's march from Spain to Italy some 2,200 years ago and Napoleon's invasion of Russia in 1812. Both of these visualizations were published in 1869 when Minard was a spry 88 years old.

Minard's flow map of Napoleon's invasion of Russia (Figure 2.11), unofficially titled "Napoleon's March by Minard," tells the story of Napoleon's army, particularly its size (by headcount) as it made its way from France to Russia and home again. As you read this visualization, moving left to right, the beige ribbon thins, signaling the waning of Napoleon's army from 422,000 to 100,000 as they marched east, during the winter, to Moscow. The army turned around and retreated, returning to France with a mere 10,000 men. We can move through the visualization, imagining the soldiers' journey and peril as they hiked through increasingly inhospitable and unfamiliar territory, turning around and coming home, losing more than 400,000 comrades on the way to war, cold, and disease.

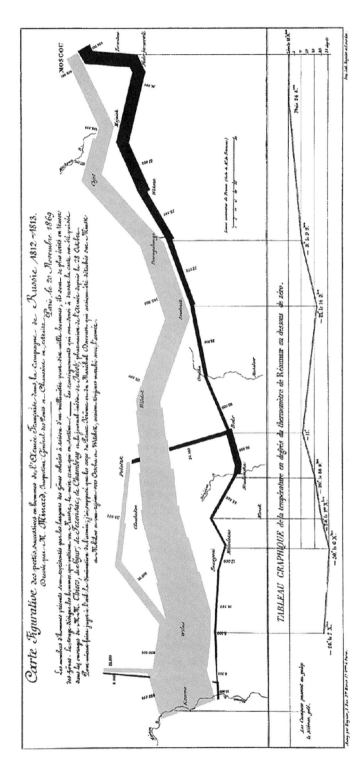

Figure 2.11   Napoleon's 1812 March by Minard, 1869.

Obviously, this was not a successful war, and as a visual analytics piece Minard's map is not a particularly successful one. However, as a visual data story around human drama, it has earned the distinction of becoming known as one of the best storytelling examples in history. You would be hard pressed to take a data visualization class today and not experience Napoleon's March. It's also fair to note that several analysts have tried to re-create it using more common statistical methods, but all fall short of the original's storytelling appeal.

Minard's second military visualization, Hannibal's journey through the Alps (not pictured), is similar in concept to Napoleon's March, although it didn't quite pull off the same memorable story. Most stories have an inherent amount of entropy—we need to tell them quickly and succinctly, and many times this means we get only one chance. In fact, numerous examples of this "once and done" effect exist in more modern visual data stories. These "one-hit wonders" are an expected consequence of good stories. Sometimes we need to tell them only once—no sequels necessary.

Story Takeaway

Stories have an inherent amount of entropy, and some we tell only once.

Stories Outside of the Box

In the discussion of Napoleon's March, we looked at a classic example of a visual data story, and with Chelsea Carson's Netflix experiment, we saw the power of modern visual analytics in action. We also looked at visual data storytelling without data in the classic sense in the two-versus-four season debate. Now, let's finish our tour of the power of visual data storytelling with one of the most quintessential instances on the books: Nigel Holmes's Monstrous Costs.

This hand-drawn illustration does exactly what a visual data story is supposed to do: transform boring data into something alive. At its core, this visualization is little more than a bar chart that shows rising costs on political campaign expenditures, but it's the storytelling detail that gives it the flair that has made it such a powerful example. The monster weaves a story around the data, anthropomorphizing these costs from dollars and cents into a ravenous beast, replete with jagged teeth and flying spittle (both of which introduce "chart junk" and perception errors, which we'll discuss later). As with the Napoleon's March by Minard graph, we'll take a much closer and more critical look at this story in a later chapter, but for now the lesson is simply that visual stories come in all shapes and sizes—some more technical looking, others so unique and personalized that they are barely recognizable as visualizations. To see more of Nigel Holmes' work, visit www.nigelholmes.com.

What skilled storytellers do is straddle that balance and capitalize on the best features to tell their story. In Monstrous Costs, these features allow the image to hook into memory, clearly telling the story of rising campaign costs with the intended emotion of the storyteller.

Story Takeaway
Don't be afraid to try something new.

Summary

In this chapter, we discussed what makes stories so impactful on the human brain. We then looked at a few real-life examples of visual data storytelling in action, both old and new. We could analyze many more examples for this purpose, and we'll continue to do so as we get hands-on with visual analytics throughout the course of this book.

Now, let's get ready to put this information to work in Tableau. In the next chapter, we'll begin exploring the Tableau ecosystem and take a journey through its freshly redesigned user interface. This will form the basis for later hands-on practice as we get to work with visual analytics and start exploring and analyzing data to build complete data visualizations and visual data stories.

CHAPTER 3

GETTING STARTED WITH TABLEAU

Application requires an environment for practice as a first step toward efficacy. This chapter shifts the focus from theory to implementation as we briefly explore the different products contained within the Tableau application suite, focusing on the Tableau Desktop 2022 user interface. We cover how to get started with Tableau Desktop, review the tool's user interface and basic functionality, and discuss how to connect to data and ensure it is properly prepared for analysis. From here, you will be able to move on to the visual analytics process to curate visuals and create data dashboards and stories, while building skills and competencies in the market-leading data visualization tool most in demand by today's employers.

While this text should not be approached as a user manual for Tableau, if you are already an intermediate Tableau user and familiar with the 2022 interface and Tableau terminology, you might want to skip this chapter and move on to Chapter 4, "Keeping Visual Analytics in Context."

Using Tableau

Acquired in June 2019 by Salesforce at a price tag of USD $15.7 billion in enterprise value,[1] Tableau stands out against other data visualization tools on the market as the industry-leading, best-of-breed tool that delivers an approachable, intuitive environment for self-service users of all levels to prepare, analyze, and visualize their data. This software also provides delivery channels for the fruits of its users' visual analysis, including dashboards and native storytelling functionality, called "story points" in Tableau. While focused on building a data-driven culture in analytics, Tableau boasts a robust and diverse data community, customer-focused innovation, an intuitive user experience, and an ever-growing catalog of enablement resources to support each of its products. As of 2022, Tableau had enjoyed a decade ranked as a Leader in Gartner's Magic Quadrant™ for Analytics and Business Intelligence Platforms (Figure 3.1).

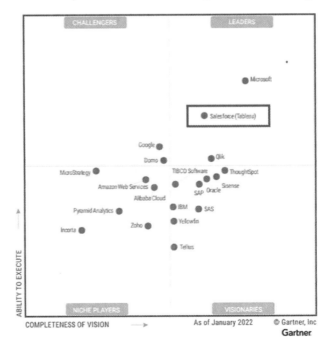

Figure 3.1 Tableau remains a Leader in the 2022 Gartner Magic Quadrant™.

Source: Gartner, March 2022.

---

1. https://investor.salesforce.com/press-releases/press-release-details/2019/Salesforce-Signs-Definitive-Agreement-to-Acquire-Tableau/default.aspx

According to Gartner's Magic Quadrant™, "Leaders demonstrate a solid understanding of the key product capabilities and the commitment to customer success that buyers in this market demand. They couple this understanding and commitment with an easily comprehensible and attractive pricing model that supports proof of value, incremental purchases, and enterprise scale. In the modern ABI platform market, buying decisions are made, or at least heavily influenced, by business users who demand products that are easy to buy and use. They require these products to deliver clear business value and enable the use of powerful analytics by those with limited technical expertise and without upfront involvement from the IT department or technical experts. In a rapidly evolving market featuring constant innovation, Leaders do not focus solely on current execution. Each also ensures it has a robust roadmap to solidify its position as a market leader and thus helps protect buyers' investments."[2]

Why Tableau?

Tableau's stated mission is to help analysts "see and understand" their data, focusing on enabling "powerful analytics for everyone." To facilitate this, the company offers a suite of software products designed to meet the needs of a diverse group of users, from experienced analysts at enterprise-level organizations to academic users, data journalists, and other visual data storytellers who want to visualize data. All Tableau products excel at displaying data visually, using Tableau's proprietary VizQL technology to enable an intuitive, drag-and-drop canvas on top of embedded and augmented analytics.

Our primary tool to apply the lessons learned in this book, Tableau Desktop can connect to a wide variety of data, stored in a variety of places on-premises or in the cloud—from SQL databases to local spreadsheets, and even many cloud database sources, such as those offered by Google Analytics, Amazon Redshift, and Salesforce. Although Tableau can mimic Excel by providing the capability to analyze rows and columns of numbers, its focus is on interactive, visual data exploration through its out-of-the-box analytic capabilities as well as dashboarding and storytelling features—no programming required. For more advanced users, Tableau offers augmented analytics powered by artificial intelligence (AI) and machine learning (ML) to streamline time to

2. Gartner.com.

insight through statistics, natural language, and smart data prep, as well as predictive modeling and other data science techniques. Data scientists can integrate and visualize results from R, Python, Einstein Discovery, MATLAB, and other extensions to scale models. Content created in Tableau Desktop can be shared in a variety of methods, depending on the user's specific needs.

> **note**
>
> Tableau Exchange is a "one-stop shop" for offerings to jumpstart your Tableau analysis, get answers to questions, and activate data quickly. Further information about accelerators, dashboard extensions, and connecters for Tableau Desktop can be accessed at exchange.tableau.com.

> **note**
>
> Tableau maintains an expansive, ongoing program to rapidly develop product features. This text attempts to capture product updates that affect fundamental learners in versions 2022.3 and 2022.4.

Founded in 2003 by an Academy Award–winning professor, a computer scientist from one of the world's most prestigious universities, and a data-passionate business leader,[3] Tableau has become synonymous with data visualization in today's analytics space. In the years since its inception, it has moved beyond a tool to become a required specialized software skill—and one that is at the top of the list for many employers. As described in a 2019 paper published by *IEEE Computer Graphics and Applications*, my fellow researchers and I mined data from Labor Insight (Burning Glass), an analytics software company powered by the largest and most sophisticated database of labor market data, in an effort to analyze data visualization–related IT job descriptions posted between March 2017 and February 2018 across the United States. In the nearly 31,000 such jobs posted within that time frame, Tableau ranked as the second most in-demand specialized software skill for visual analysts (42% of such listings), outranked only by SQL.[4] When the same study was repeated in 2022, in the data visualization–related IT job descriptions posted between March 2021 and March 2022, Tableau remained the second most in-demand specialized software skill (once again behind SQL), now being mentioned in 48% of those listings (Figure 3.2).

---

3. www.tableau.com/about

4. Ryan, L.; Silver, D.; Laramee, R.; & Purdue, D. "Teaching Data Visualization as a Skill." *IEEE Computer Graphics and Applications* 39, no. 2 (2019): 95–103.

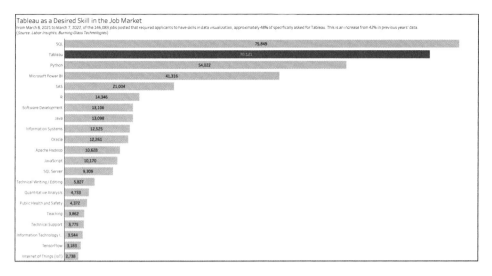

Tableau as a Desired Skill in the Job Market
From March 8, 2021 to March 7, 2022, of the 146,083 jobs posted that required applicants to have skills in data visualization, approximately 48% of specifically asked for Tableau. This is an increase from 42% in previous years' data.
(*Source: Labor Insights, Burning Glass Technologies*)

Figure 3.2 From March 8, 2021, to March 7, 2022, of the 146,083 jobs posted that required applicants to have skills in data visualization, approximately 48% of specifically asked for Tableau.

TABLEAU IN DEMAND

In a recent analysis of Labor Insight (Burning Glass), approximately 146,038 jobs posted across the United States between March 1, 2021, and March 31, 2022. listed "data visualization" as a desirable skill. Among the most popular job titles were data analyst (6.4%), data scientist (5.9%), and BI analyst (2.6%). These findings are consistent with previous years' research, although the data scientist job title has now edged above BI analyst. All postings required, at a minimum, a bachelor's degree.

In addition to Tableau, other high-ranking software skills included Microsoft Office Suite (not including PowerBI; 113,000 jobs), SQL (76,000 jobs), Python (54,000 jobs), SAS (21,000 jobs), and R (14,000 jobs). When pitted against the intersection of other required baseline "soft" skills, those listed included communications (75,000 jobs), teamwork/collaboration (63,000 jobs), research (53,000 jobs), and problem solving (49,000 jobs). A separate but similar study found that the term "storytelling" is also making its mark on jobs in visual analytics, with 7,451 of 146,038 job postings, or 5.1%, also looking for qualified candidates experienced in data storytelling.

These analysis results are consistent with recent surveys that have looked at which tools are most in demand and in use by today's visual analytics practitioners. One such resource is the Data Visualization Society's State of the Industry (SOTU) report, discussed in Chapter 1. Its 2021 survey marked the first year that respondents were asked which technologies they use *often*—rather than the more general question used previously, which simply asked about tools used, but did not differentiate between which tools were used on a regular basis versus used at all. Regardless, the top tools mentioned by respondents have remained consistent over the years the DVS has conducted this survey, with Tableau coming in second only to Excel. Interestingly, 2021 also marked the emergence of PowerPoint as a data visualization tool, based on 2020 write-ins for "other" in regard to tools used to proliferate results to stakeholders and other visualization audiences.

If you're wondering where these data visualization jobs are located, nearly 15% were in California, just shy of 10% in the New York/New Jersey metro area, and another 8% in Texas. Washington, home to Tableau's Seattle headquarters, accounted for fewer than 4% of the jobs. Note that these percentages are based on the count of total jobs posted and are not normalized for population. Top employers included PricewaterhouseCoopers, Deloitte, Humana, and Amazon.

The Tableau Product Portfolio

It's important to think of Tableau as a brand, rather than a product. The Tableau ecosystem includes several different products, and although Tableau Desktop is its cornerstone data visualization software product and the focus of this book, other environments are also offered in the Tableau application suite to support various levels of user needs. What unites all of these products is VizQL, Tableau's proprietary visual technology that enables simple drag-and-drop functions to create sophisticated visualizations. The primary differences between these core products are the different data sources users can connect to (connectivity), how visualizations can be shared with others (distribution), the ability to automatically update or refresh analysis (automation), and the level of governance required by the user and/or organization (security).

note

VizQL is Tableau's proprietary analysis technology. You can read more about VizQL at www.tableau.com/products/technology.

Tableau Desktop

Tableau's flagship product, Tableau Desktop, is an application that can be installed on either Windows or Mac machines. It allows connection to data on premises or in the cloud, and facilitates the entire visual discovery and analytics process from connecting to data to sharing visualizations, dashboards, and interactive stories using Tableau Server and Tableau Cloud. The software also includes a device designer to help users design and publish dashboards optimized for various form factors. Tableau Desktop enables users with intuitive visual analytics experiences and augmented analytics (powered by AI and ML). Advanced analysts can also integrate and visualize results from R, Python, Einstein Discovery, MATLAB, and other extensions.

note

Work in this book, in terms of both hands-on work and the figures presented throughout, relies on Tableau Desktop version 2022, unless otherwise stated. A number of features are consistent across Tableau Desktop, Server, and Cloud, but their functionality does differ. If you are not already an active Tableau user, it's recommended that you download Tableau Desktop to follow along with the discussion. Information on Tableau's free trial offerings can be found in the Introduction.

Tableau Server

From small businesses to *Fortune* 500 companies, Tableau Server extends the value of data across the entire organization for enterprise-wide deployments and is intended for organization-wide provision of visual analytics outputs through a central repository for Tableau work. It provides organizations with centralized governance, visibility, and control, while allowing users to curate, publish, and share data sources as well as collaborate, engage, and explore data. Data visualizations and dashboards are typically stored within the organization.

Tableau Cloud

Formerly called Tableau Online, Tableau Cloud is a full-hosted, cloud-based, enterprise-grade solution. It provides similar functionality as Tableau Server, but has the advantages of cloud distribution and automation and is hosted off premises.

Tableau Prep

Tableau's newest offering, Tableau Prep provides a modern approach to data preparation. Tableau Prep can connect to data on premises or in the cloud, and provides robust data preparation capabilities using Tableau's familiar visual interface. Outputs can be opened in Tableau Desktop, Server, or Cloud to fit seamlessly into an analytic workflow, reducing friction between data prep and analysis.

Tableau Public

One part data visualization hosting service, one part social networking, Tableau Public is a free service that allows users to publish interactive data visualizations online. These visualizations can be embedded into websites and blogs, shared via social media or email, or made available for download to other users, but must remain in Tableau's public cloud.

> note
>
> You can follow me and see many of the visualizations included in this book on Tableau Public at https://public.tableau.com/app/profile/lindy.ryan.

Tableau Reader and Tableau Viewer

Finally, Tableau offers two products that allow anyone, from experienced users to casual users, to access and interact with content created by Tableau creators. While both products are similar, they do have some notable differences.

Tableau Reader

Tableau Reader is a free desktop application that allows users to open and interact with data visualizations built in Tableau Desktop in a view-only mode (or, conversely, to distribute content built in Tableau Desktop). Tableau Reader lacks governance, security, and administration capabilities, so it is not possible for users to make any changes to visualizations provided in Tableau Reader. Thus, the application is essentially a distribution platform with no analytic capabilities.

Tableau Viewer

Tableau Viewer is a role-based license option on Tableau Server that allows users to access and interact with trusted content without putting the security of data at risk. Tableau Viewer users benefit from the security of a governed server-based deployment and can actively engage, interact, and collaborate with shared content.

> **note**
>
> See Appendix A, "Tableau Services," to learn about the range of services that Tableau offers to support your ongoing learning related to visual data analytics as well as the Tableau ecosystem.

GETTING SOCIAL WITH TABLEAU MOBILE

While Tableau Desktop natively includes many sharing capabilities (primarily through exporting or posting to Tableau Public), Tableau Server and Cloud users benefit from Tableau Mobile, a companion app that gives your audience access to your Tableau site on the go. The app is available for Android and iOS and allows your audience to interact with published visual content and discover data insights—even offline. Once you share content, recipients receive a notification and shared content appears in the "Shared with Me" channel on their home screen. Desktop users can also publish content to Tableau Server or Cloud, if this feature is enabled by their organization, by using the Share icon on the toolbar.

Learn more about Tableau Mobile at www.tableau.com/products/mobile.

Getting Started

To begin working in Tableau Desktop, the first thing you need to do is get your hands on a license. If you have not done so already, refer to the Introduction for guidance on how to start a free trial of Tableau Desktop. You can also visit the Tableau website to explore trial and purchase options. As previously noted, all exercises and tutorials contained in this book use Tableau Desktop 2022.

Installing Tableau Desktop

Before installing Tableau Desktop, make sure your machine meets the necessary requirements for the application. Tableau Desktop is available for Windows and Mac, and the minimum requirements as of this book's writing were as follows:

- **Windows Operating Systems**
  - Microsoft Windows 8/8.1, Windows 10 (x64)
  - 2 GB memory
  - 1.5 GB minimum free desk space
  - CPUs must support SSE4.2 and POPCNT instruction sets

- **Mac Operating Systems**
  - macOS Mojave 10.14, macOS Catalina 10.15, and Big Sur 11.4+
  - Intel processors
  - M1 processors under Rosetta 2 emulation mode
  - 1.5 GB minimum free disk space
  - CPUs must support SSE4.2 and POPCNT instruction sets

> note
>
> Research these and other minimum system requirements at www.tableau.com/products/techspecs.

Connecting to Data

When you first open Tableau Desktop, the Connect to Data screen appears (Figure 3.3). This "starting screen" is the first thing users see after launching the Tableau software.

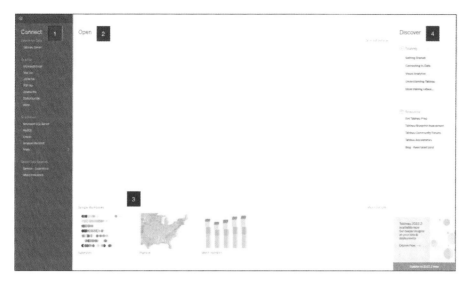

Figure 3.3 The Tableau Connect to Data screen.

There are several important elements to know on this screen:

- **Connect:** All possible data connections can be accessed here to connect to your data, including those stored locally or on servers. Additionally, two saved data sources—Sample-Superstore and World Indicators—are training data sets included natively within Tableau.

- **Open:** As you create your own workbooks, recently opened workbooks appear here for quick access.

- **Sample Workbooks:** Similarly to the saved data sources, these are default workbook samples provided by Tableau that can be used as simulations for training or other skills development. (Note: Beginning in Tableau 2022.4, these sample workbooks are now termed *Accelerators*.)

- **Discover:** This pane connects you to various Tableau training, visualization, and other resources. Announcements for upcoming Tableau events, Viz of the Day, and upgrade reminders also appear at the bottom of this pane.

> note
>
> This book focuses on the fundamentals of practicing visual analytics within the scope of data visualization and visual data storytelling; it is *not* a user manual for Tableau. For more granular learning on Tableau, review the Training videos provided by Tableau in the Discover pane or the resources listed in Appendix A of this book.

Connecting to Tables

Selecting a saved data source from the Connect pane will immediately take you to the Tableau worksheet canvas, bypassing the data preparation stage. We'll review this interface later in this chapter, but first let's take a look at how to prepare your data for analysis in Tableau.

> **Tip**
>
> For many exercises in this book, we'll use the Sample-Superstore training file provided on the Saved Data Resources section of the Connect to Data screen shown in Figure 3.3. It is a well-prepared, simple dataset for a global retailer that sells furniture, office supplies, and technology goods. You can connect to this data source simply by double-clicking on it on the Connect pane. We will also use an Excel-based dataset called Global Superstore, which contains similar but not the same data. This dataset, and others, can be downloaded by visiting the resources provided in the Introduction and Appendix A of this book.

For our purposes, we'll connect to a very common file format—an Excel spreadsheet. You can connect to any Excel spreadsheet by clicking the Excel option under the Connect menu and navigating to the file's location on your machine. Once connected to your data file (or any other file or database connection), Tableau opens the Data Source page (Figure 3.4).

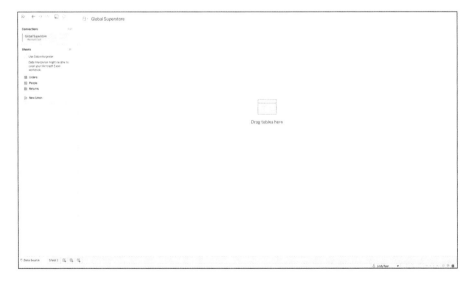

Figure 3.4 The Data Source page.

Before we look at options to make changes to the data at this point, it's important to note that whatever changes are made create metadata and have no impact on the underlying data source. This means you can make specific changes and prepare data directly in Tableau without affecting the data's existing infrastructure.

The Data Source page provides several options to help you prepare this file for analysis in Tableau.

- **Connections:** You can add additional data sources by clicking Add. You can also edit the name of the connection or remove it as desired by clicking the drop-down arrow to the right of the filename. (You can also rename the connection by clicking its title on the canvas to the right.)
- **Sheets:** This pane displays all the sheets in the Excel file, corresponding to the names of individual worksheet tabs. Sheets in Excel are treated the same as tables in a database, and you can choose to connect to a single table or join multiple tables. To connect to a sheet, simply drag and drop it into the data connection canvas to the right (you will notice a "Drag tables here" prompt) or by double-clicking the sheet desired. After you connect to a sheet, three things happen (Figure 3.5), which allow you to further explore the capabilities of this screen:
    - The sheet name appears in the data connection canvas.
    - The data is displayed in the preview pane below the data connection canvas.
    - A Go To Worksheet icon is displayed.

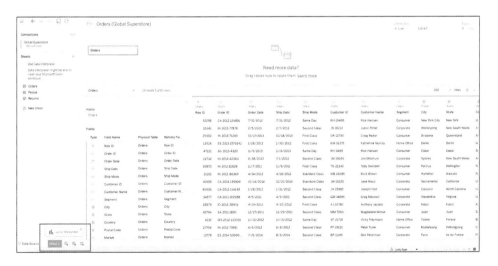

Figure 3.5 You have connected to the Orders table of the Excel file, populating the data preview pane. Tableau also provides the prompt to Go To Worksheet, which allows you to begin visually exploring the data if you are ready.

Before moving on, there are a few more things to take note of on this screen.

First, if you aren't satisfied with any individual column name, you can click the drop-down arrow to the right of the name and select Rename. Additionally, clicking the data type icon allows you to change the default data type for that column (Figure 3.6).

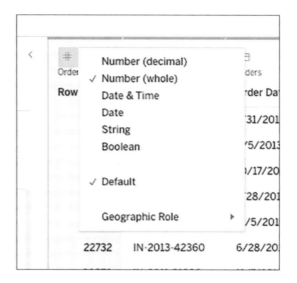

Figure 3.6 Clicking the data type icon allows you to change the default data type for that column. This determines how the fields are displayed on your worksheet in the next step.

If you would like to further refine your columnar data, you can find a few more options to prepare this data by clicking the drop-down arrow on the column (Figure 3.7):

- Rename the field.
- Copy values.
- Hide (or show) fields.
- Assign new names to individual dimension members via an Alias.
- Create calculated fields to create a new field before populating your Tableau worksheet.
- Create groups to combine different dimension members.
- Split fields by delimiter using an automatic or custom split. (Note: This option appears only if the data can be split.)

- Pivot data fields as necessary. (Note: You can do only one data pivot per data source.)

- The Describe option gives you additional information about the field.

Depending on the data type contained within the field, some options may not be available. Likewise, for quantitative fields, the string functions are not available, but an additional option, Create Bins, allows you to create equally sized bins—an ability useful for making histograms.

Figure 3.7 Clicking the drop-down arrow provides more options to prepare data.

Live Versus Extract

You might have noticed the option for a Live or Extract connection on the sheet canvas (Figure 3.8).

Figure 3.8 Options for connecting live or extracting data.

By default, most data sources will connect live with no filters. However, before you begin analyzing data, this decision might be something you want to consider. Be sure to understand the benefits and drawbacks of Live versus Extract connection options as described in Table 3.1.

Table 3.1   Pros and cons of Live versus Extract connection options

Connection	Pros	Cons
Live	• Leverage a high-performance database's capabilities. • See real-time changes in data. • Offers the best security in most organizations.	• Can result in a slower experience. • Some cloud-based data sources must be extracted.
Extract	• Can deter latency in a slow database. • Could reduce the query load on critical systems.	• Most Online Analytical Processing (OLAP) data sources cannot be extracted. • Must be refreshed periodically.

Finally, you have the ability to filter the entire data source before working with it in Tableau. These filters can be created with any combination of fields by clicking the blue Add text under Filters. Filtering may help eliminate clutter or extraneous fields by streamlining your view of the data and removing data that is not needed for analysis.

Connecting to Multiple Tables with Relationships and Joins

As mentioned earlier, you can connect to multiple data sources in Tableau. You can also connect to multiple tables in the same data source. Previously, connecting multiple tables, or data sources, in Tableau was achieved through joins. However, starting in Tableau 2020.2, a new logical layer was added to Tableau's data model, improving this functionality. While joins are still an option to connect multiple tables, this new logical layer uses "relationships" to normalize data sources with multiple tables at a different level of detail.

Relationships are a dynamic, flexible way to combine data for analysis, and generally a simpler process than working with joins. Therefore, Tableau recommends using relationships as a first approach to combining data.

To create a relationship, drag and drop or double-click the second sheet to which you want to connect. A "noodle" appears (Figure 3.9), which represents the relationship between the selected tables. Tableau automatically attempts to choose related fields, but users can manually adjust these—or choose another set of related fields.

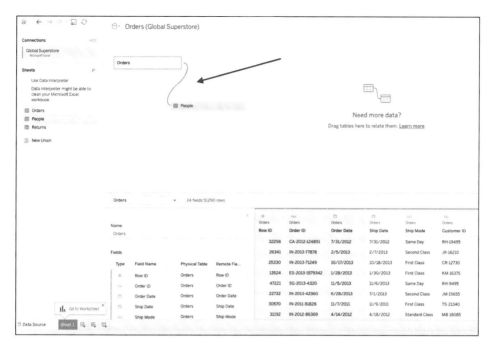

Figure 3.9 The relationship "noodle."

The data grid displays columns for each table, depending on which is selected on the upper pane. Although relationships do not merge tables together, Tableau automatically configures the join type, the right aggregation, and the handling of null values.

Relationships aside, there may be times when you still opt to create a join. To create a join, double-click on the first table, then drag out the second table. This will generate the same join experience as in previous versions of Tableau via the join canvas (Figure 3.10).

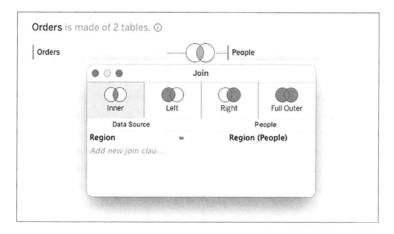

Figure 3.10 The join canvas.

The join icon with the blue center indicates that Tableau has automatically joined these tables as an inner join, making it the default join clause. Clicking the join icon will display the details and give you the option to edit the join clause, or even create a new one.

While Tableau will automatically join your tables, it does so by guessing your matching ID. You can change this default by clicking on the fields, which shows a drop-down menu of all data fields available to join.

Overview of Join Types

Tableau provides four types of joins that you can use to combine your data: inner, left, right, and outer. Inner and left joins are the most common types of joins.

- **Inner join:** Joins records where there is a matching field in both datasets. Using an inner join to combine tables produces a new virtual table that contains values that have matches in both tables.

- **Left join:** Joins records from the left and right sides of your equation when there is a match. Using a left join to combine tables produces a new virtual table that contains all values from the left table and corresponding matches from the right table. When there is no corresponding match from left to right, you will see a null value.

- **Right join:** Joins all the records from the data on the right side of your equation and any matching records from the left side. The opposite of a left join, using a right join to combine tables produces a table that contains all values from the right table and corresponding matches from the left. Likewise, when a value in the right table doesn't have a corresponding match in the left table, you will see a null value.

- **Outer join:** Joins all the records from each dataset together, even when there is no join (this option is rarely used). Using a full outer join to combine tables produces a table that contains all values from both tables. If a value from either table doesn't have a match with the other table, you will see a null value.

WHAT ARE "NULLS"?

Occasionally as you work with data, you will discover a field name called null. What is that?

Null means that your data contains some empty cells and Tableau is, essentially, letting you know about their presence. These fields could have been left blank—either intentionally or unintentionally—or they may signify missing or unknown values. Checking fields and formatting for extraneous information is always important when doing data analysis because you want to ensure these blank fields do not skew the results. A null field might indicate an error in the data or some other inaccuracy. When null values exist in a connected dataset, Tableau displays an indicator that provides options to filter out these unknown values. We'll take a closer look at working with nulls in a later chapter.

ABOUT TABLEAU PREP

A relatively recent addition to the Tableau application suite, Tableau Prep is a separate product designed to make preparing data easy and intuitive. Expanding data preparation capabilities beyond those available in Data Interpreter, Tableau Prep can help you combine, shape, and clean your data for analysis in Tableau. As an additional tool, Tableau Prep is only lightly covered in this book. More in-depth information can be found at www.tableau.com/products/prep.

Adding and Replacing Data Sources

Sometimes, you might want to work with multiple data sources in the same Tableau workbook without joining or otherwise blending the data. Luckily, Tableau offers some options for performing this type of analysis—including recent feature updates in Tableau 2022.4 that make this process more seamless and flexible than ever before.

Once you've connected to your primary data source as usual, navigate to your worksheet. This worksheet will automatically utilize data from your first data source.

From here, use the top menu bar to select Data > New Data Source (Figure 3.11). You can then use the familiar Connect to Data screen to select and connect to your additional data source and, if needed, navigate to the Data Connection canvas to see and select fields for use as the new data source.

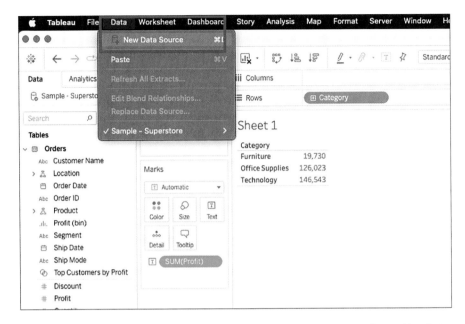

Figure 3.11 To add or replace data sources, first use the top menu bar to select Data > New Data Source.

Once this process is complete, you will be able to see all connected data sources in the Data pane on your Tableau worksheet (Figure 3.12).

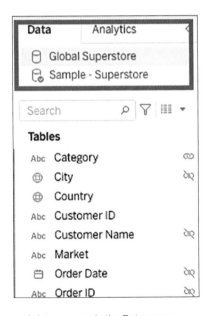

Figure 3.12 Review all connected data sources in the Data pane.

From here, as you begin to explore and analyze your data, you can selectively replace data sources at the worksheet level (in the past, replacing data sources would apply to all worksheets in the Tableau workbook). To replace the data set used, return to the Data menu and select Data > Replace Data Source. This option enables you to replace the data source with any other connected data source, at either the worksheet or workbook level (Figure 3.13).

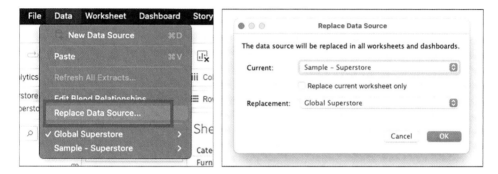

Figure 3.13 Data sources can be changed at either the workbook or worksheet level.

Basic Data Prep with Data Interpreter

Tableau Desktop delivers some features to help automatically reshape files to get them ready for analysis in Tableau without relying on additional tools (such as Tableau Prep) or other data prep tools. One is Data Interpreter, Tableau's built-in tool for preparing data for analysis. While many of the Excel files we'll use in this text are already nicely formatted and ready for analysis in Tableau, real-world data files are not always so well prepared. If you need to connect to a data table where minimal amounts of data prep is necessary, Data Interpreter is a handy resource.

When you connect to an Excel sheet in Tableau, the software can recognize issues such as missing column names, null values, and so on. To remedy these problems and clean the file for use in analysis, Tableau will suggest using Data Interpreter. (Refer to Figure 3.4 to locate the Data Interpreter option on the left pane of Data Source screen, directly between the list of data connections and the resultant tables.)

We will take a closer look at Data Interpreter in a later chapter, but for now it's sufficient to know that to use Data Interpreter, you simply click the check box to activate this tool. This executes a query to the Excel file and confirms its automated prep tasks, with a revised data preview pane addressing the issues Data Interpreter has identified. To get more specifics on what Data Interpreter has adjusted in the file, including a before-and-after view and an explanation table, click the link that is provided following Data Interpreter's action to "Review the results." This opens an Excel file describing the changes. You can also clear the check box to undo these changes and revert to your original sheet.

After verifying the changes made to your data, you can go to your worksheet and begin exploring the Tableau interface and your data. You are ready to begin your analysis!

Navigating the Tableau Interface

Now that you have connected to some data in Tableau, you can click the prompt to Go To Worksheet and start getting to know the Tableau user interface (UI) in a more meaningful way. Like the Data Source page, the Tableau UI is a drag-and-drop interface that fosters rich interactivity between sheets, dashboards, and stories, allowing for in-depth visual exploration and powerful visual communication. Tableau is similar to Excel in that its files are called workbooks and the sheets inside the workbook are called sheets. Every Tableau workbook contains three elements:

- **Sheets:** For creating individual visualizations. Each workbook can contain multiple sheets—one for each data visualization you create.
- **Dashboards:** For combining multiple sheets as well as other objects like images, text, and web pages, and adding interactions between them like filtering and highlighting. Dashboards are great for looking at the interactions between multiple visualizations in a single view.
- **Stories:** These frameworks can be based on visualizations or dashboards, or they can be based on different views and explorations of a single visualization, seen at different stages, with different marks filtered and annotations added. However, stories are best suited to narrate the story in your data.

We'll cover dashboards and stories, and the differences between them, in more depth in later chapters. For now, let's focus on sheets and take a high-level view of the various areas of the Tableau worksheet canvas. As we begin to work directly with data to perform visual analytics and build visualizations, dashboards, and stories throughout this book, we'll explore these areas—and more—in detail through hands-on exercises. For now, this high-level overview is intended to orient you to the various aspects of the user interface.

As shown in Figure 3.14, the Tableau interface includes five basic elements:

1. Menus and toolbar
2. Data pane
3. Shelves and cards

4. The canvas workspace

5. Legends

Figure 3.14 The Tableau user interface, a blank canvas.

Menus and Toolbar

Even though most of your Tableau work can be accomplished by interacting directly with the drag-and-drop canvas, the menu bar that launches with the software includes various menus that provide access to additional features and settings. This includes the File and Data menus, as well as the Worksheet, Dashboard, and Story menus, each of which contains specific controls for those canvas types. Additional menus, such as the Analysis, Map, Format, Server, Windows, and Help menus, contain even more functionality and controls.

At the top of the Tableau sheet is the toolbar, which is similar in concept to the ribbon in Microsoft Office products. The toolbar contains many powerful buttons that give you control over your Tableau experience and enable you to navigate from the data source all the way to story presentation mode. A few items of special note are highlighted here:

- **Logo:** The Tableau logo button brings you back to the original Connect to Data screen (clicking the icon from this screen returns you to your sheet).

- **Undo:** There is no limit to how much you can undo in Tableau, which is an important feature for exploration and discovery. The icon is grayed out until there is an action to undo.

- **Save:** There is *no automatic save* in Tableau. Be sure to save your work incrementally.

Another menu appears along the bottom of the sheet. This menu, similar in concept to a Tableau workbook, enables you to return to the Data Source screen; create new sheets, dashboards, or stories; and do things like rename, rearrange, duplicate, delete various sheets, and so on.

Data Pane

The pane on the left of the sheet is called the Data pane. It has two tabs: a Data tab and an Analytics tab.

Data

At the top of the Data tab is a list of all open data connections and the fields from that data source categorized as either dimensions or measures (discussed shortly).

Analytics

The Analytics tab enables you to bring out pieces of your analysis—summaries, models, and more—as drag-and-drop elements. We will review these functions later.

Shelves and Cards

Shelves and cards are some of the most dynamic and useful features of the Tableau UI.

- **Columns and Rows shelves:** Control grouping headers (dimensions) and axes (measures).
- **Pages shelf:** Lets you break a view into a series of pages so you can better analyze how a specific field affects the rest of the data.
- **Filters shelf:** Filters visualizations by dimensions or measures.
- **Marks card:** Controls the visual characteristics of a visualization, including encoding of color, size, labels, tooltip text, and shape.
- **"Show Me" card** (shown closed): A collapsible card that shows application visualization types for a selected measure and dimension.

Legends

Legends will be created and automatically appear when you place a field on the Color, Size, or Shape card. To change the order (or appearance) of fields in a visualization, drag them around in the legend. Hide legends by clicking on the menu and selecting Hide Card. Likewise, bring them back by selecting the Legend option on the appropriate space in the Marks card or by using the Analysis menu.

Understanding Dimensions and Measures

When you bring a data source into Tableau, the software automatically classifies each field as either a dimension or a measure. The differences between these two are important, though they can be tricky to understand for those who are new at analytics. Perhaps the best way to differentiate these two classifications is to think about them this way: Dimensions are categories, whereas measures are fields you can do math with.

Dimensions

Dimensions are things that you can use to group data by or drill down by. They are usually, but not always, categories (e.g., City, Product Name, or Color), and they can be logically grouped into strings, dates, or geographic fields. Dimensions can also be organized into Tableau groups and hierarchies, which we'll discuss shortly.

Measures

Measures are generally numerical data on which you want to perform calculations—summing, averaging, and so on. The definition of a field as a measure or dimension can be adjusted in the Data Source screen by clicking the data type icon. You can also change this directly in the sheet by either dragging and dropping a dimension to measure, and vice versa, or by clicking the drop-down menu by any field and selecting the Convert to Measure (or Dimension) option.

Continuous and Discrete

Generally, dimensions are discrete, whereas measures are continuous. We could break this down a little more into four types or levels of measurement:

- **Nominal measures** are discrete and categorical (e.g., for/against, true/false, yes/no).
- **Ordinal measures** have order but there are not distinct, equal values (e.g., rankings).
- **Interval measures** have order and distinct, equal values—or at least we assume they are equal (e.g., Likert scales).
- **Ratio measures** have order, distinct/equal values, and a true zero point (e.g., length, weight).

In Tableau, continuous fields produce axes, whereas discrete fields create headers. Continuous means "forming an unbroken whole, without interruption." Discrete means "individually separate and distinct." Be sure you understand the difference between these mathematical terms. Text and categories (dimensions) are inherently discrete. Numbers can be discrete if they can take only one of a limited set of distinct, separate values (e.g., a rating). Numbers, including dates, can be continuous if they can take on any value in a range.

COLORFUL PILLS

When a field is brought from the Data pane and dropped into the Rows and Columns shelves, Tableau creates a "pill." These pills are color coded: Blue pills represent discrete variables, whereas green pills are continuous. The data type icons also reflect these color codes (Figure 3.15).

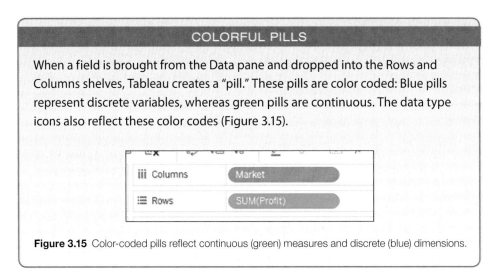

Figure 3.15 Color-coded pills reflect continuous (green) measures and discrete (blue) dimensions.

Summary

This chapter introduced the Tableau product ecosystem. It then took a high-level view of the Tableau user interface, including connecting and preparing data and the core functionality of the Sheets canvas. In future chapters, you will put this knowledge into practice as you begin working hands-on with this functionality.

The next chapter addresses the importance of context in visual analytics.

CHAPTER 4

KEEPING VISUAL ANALYTICS IN CONTEXT

This chapter describes the importance of understanding data's context and its role in helping visual analysts ask the right questions to build a data narrative framework. You'll learn about exploratory and explanatory analysis and strategies for successful data storytelling, including narrative flow, considerations for spoken versus written narratives that support visuals, and structures that can support your stories for maximum impact. We'll also explore helpful techniques in Tableau that can guide you in crafting effective data narrative structures and keeping data firmly connected to its context.

More than 20 years ago, Bill Gates coined the iconic phrase, "Content is king." Gates was, of course, referring to the importance of content on demand in the early days (circa 1996) of the World Wide Web. His words were prophetic, however, and over the past two-plus decades this mantra has been applied to everything from Internet marketing to media journalists to viral content creators online—suddenly *everyone* is a media company.

The never-ending quest for bigger, bolder, better online content has radically changed the way people acquire and share information and how we interact and communicate with others. However, although Gates might have been right when he made his proclamation, his mantra is missing a critical ingredient: context.

If you type Gates's "content is king" into your Google search bar, you might notice that a "but" is coming right behind it (Figure 4.1). Content is king, but context is god.

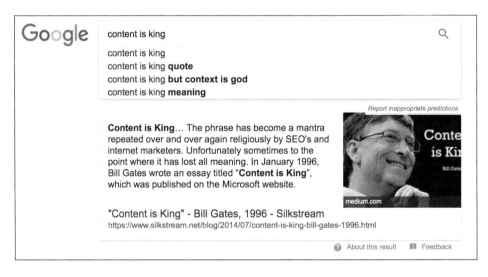

Figure 4.1 Sorry, Bill. Content might be king, but context is god.

Context is especially important in visual analytics. Just as communication begins before you ever start building your first data visualization, like any good story, a visual data story requires context—a setting, a plot, and a goal—before you can begin to communicate and share insights. Discovering this context is part of the storytelling process.

As a final point before we get hands-on with visual analytics in Tableau, this chapter focuses on ensuring you understand the importance of context in crafting data visualizations and visual data stories, how to ask the right questions that will help you begin to build out your data storytelling framework, and how to let context drive the data story as you share it with your audience. The context of a data story is made up of four ingredients:

- Context of **data**
- Context of **structure**
- Context of **audience**
- Context of **presentation**

> **context caution**
>
> There's more to context than just the data. Context can also be created by the storyteller or by the audience, based on knowledge, biases, and expectations. A successful storyteller needs to learn how to anticipate these issues and ensure they do not improperly affect analysis or design. A good way to ensure your context works for you, rather than against you, is to ask and then answer a series of logically thought-out and connected questions about the project, the data, and the audience. The answers to these questions help provide a framework for your data story.

Context in Action

To quote football consulting company 21st Club, without context (in analytics), data is "meaningless, irrelevant, and even dangerous."[1] This might sound aggressive, but in practice, it's an understatement. Without context, we can't answer any of the pivotal journalistic questions—who, what, where, when, why, and how—that provide pertinent details to help us get to the bottom of any big question. In fact, we can't do much beyond just make good guesses—not an effective strategy in analytics. We have a whole lot of information, but without context, it is incomplete. This can cause us to miss out on major points that change the entire scope of our story. Beyond just-plain-bad storytelling, omitting critical context carries an even bigger risk. Ultimately, we use visual analytics to drive decision making, and nothing paves the way for bad decisions like a lack of good information.

Let's take a quick look at a fun example of a story where context makes all the difference.

---

1. www.21stclub.com/2013/08/11/contextual-intelligence-a-definition/

Harry Potter: Hero or Menace?

In January 2022, J. K. Rowling's wizarding world celebrated its 20th anniversary with the release of *Harry Potter 20th Anniversary: Return to Hogwarts*.

By now, most of us are familiar with The Boy Who Lived and the *Harry Potter* author. To date, the franchise book series has been distributed in more than 200 territories, translated into 68 languages, and has sold more than 400 million copies worldwide.[2] There are companion volumes, a spin-off series, and a bevy of critical discourse on everything from the author's controversial tweets to the series' ongoing literary and cultural impact. There are even conferences, like the Harry Potter Academic Conference, a nonprofit annual academic conference hosted by Chestnut Hill College. However, although most of us are familiar with Harry's story through film and media, it's unlikely that we've taken a concentrated look on the data inside the story.

> note
>
> If you're a Potterhead, you're in luck! A later chapter explores several stories hidden within the Wizarding World's data—working through the entire storytelling process from collecting and preparing data to presenting a complete data narrative.

Even if you don't know all the nuances of the Wizarding World, you likely do know that the story follows the journey of young wizard Harry Potter as he fights against the dark wizard, Lord Voldemort, and his minions (known, attractively, as Death Eaters). With that minimal amount of context, we can assume that Harry is the good guy and Voldemort the bad.

To aid in visualizing the story of good versus evil in *Harry Potter*, we can use a visualization of all of the instances where characters act aggressively. When we visualize this data at the most superficial level—a count of aggressive acts enacted by Harry and Voldemort in each of the books, in order of release date—these "lightning bolts" seem to show that Harry committed significantly more aggressive behaviors than did his nemesis, Lord Voldemort, over the course of the series (Figure 4.2). In this version of the story, our good wizard suddenly looks a little more sociopathic than we might have expected. Yikes!

---

2. http://harrypotter.scholastic.com/jk_rowling/

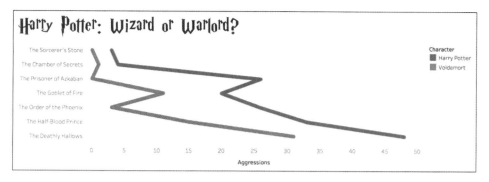

Figure 4.2 A modified bar chart of aggressive actions committed by Harry Potter and Lord Voldemort.

The good news for Potter fans is that if we look at the data like this and fail to put the count of aggressive behaviors into context, we overlook critical context and showcase a faulty story. We don't know, for example, if these "aggressive behaviors" were inciting or if they were reactionary, defensive, or protective—since these latter could themselves be labeled aggressive as well.

Remember, the danger of a story told wrong is the prospect of making a bad decision based on inaccurate or otherwise faulty information. This logic applies to any story—even Harry's. If we had presented this visual to, for example, Rowling's publisher prior to the series' publication, we might never have been introduced the Wizarding World. Who would want to publish a children's book that condones violence? Or, more aptly, who would want their children reading about a malevolent hero? In this case, telling an incorrect story could have resulted in a wrong decision (no Potter), rather than introducing a pop-culture phenomenon that swept the world.

Fortunately, we can remedy this by putting context back into the narrative. Let's try again.

Ensuring Relevant Context

To make sure we're including context in a meaningful way, we need to revisit our initial assumptions and reconsider how we contextualize two key variables: (1) the two characters and (2) their aggressive acts.

In the previous attempt, we simply visualized a count of aggressive acts and neglected to consider the context in which the acts were committed. We also failed to consider the influence of the character on the narrative. Doing so puts an undue spotlight on Harry and presents an immediate contextual fallacy. This is Harry's story, after all, and as the protagonist, his actions, aggressive or not, are heavily documented. In contrast, Voldemort, while a main character, has a lesser presence in the story. This logic helps us see critical context we neglected in our simple counting exercise. Rather than how many aggressive acts were committed by each character, we need to look at how often each character appears *and* how often they commit aggressive acts when mentioned.

- *Out of context:* How *many times* Harry and Voldemort acted aggressively.
- *In context:* How *often* Harry and Voldemort acted aggressively *when mentioned*.

This still isn't a perfect solution, as it doesn't account for *what* the aggressive action was—for example, if it was offensive or defensive. Nevertheless, putting the data into a relevant context will enable us to see something very different when we visualize the data again (Figure 4.3).

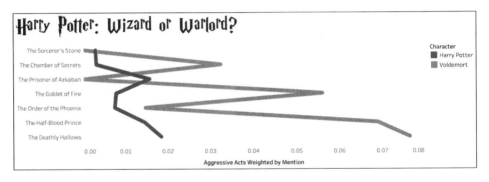

Figure 4.3 With a little bit of context added back into the data, we see a different story.

With more context added into the narrative, we see Voldemort's true colors emerge and a much more significant insight becomes apparent: While Harry *rarely* acts aggressively when mentioned, Voldemort *usually* acts aggressively when he appears on the page. This completely changes the story takeaway that we presented earlier.

Of course, there is much more exploration and analysis we could do with this data to dig deeper into the role of aggression in *Harry Potter* and craft a richer visual narrative. We could bring more characters into view to analyze whether Voldemort is the ultimate bad guy in the series. We could look at aggression by book rather than by character, or we could look at who committed aggressive acts against whom and how and when character relationships affect how these aggressions are brought into play. We could even break down aggressive acts into violent and nonviolent categories or rank aggressive acts by level of severity (which, in fact, we do in a later chapter). In any case, it's unlikely the full context of this story could ever be told without knowledge of the series and its complicated plot, and both of these require support on the part of the presenter. This hints to the value of presentation in a visual data story. No matter how deep, data alone will never be able to tell a story as well as *you*.

> note
>
> Be especially careful with *counts*, as they can influence your data and present a distorted version of the truth. To prevent this, "normalize" your data with a calculated field.

Exploratory Versus Explanatory Analysis

Before moving on to the topic of curating the outputs of visual analytics, we need to draw a distinction between exploratory and explanatory analysis and consider how they contribute to both data visualizations and visual data storytelling.

Exploration fuels discovery. It's the process we take to explore data and uncover its story. In my visual analytics classes, I use an image of Indiana Jones to illustrate the concept of exploratory analysis because, like Dr. Jones, this is where we go looking for a discovery to share and hope to find something. We take time to search, digging in and out of data iteratively and with curiosity as we work to build a story, or perhaps many stories, or perhaps even none at all. Exploration is a process of "look and see," and we must explore before we can explain.

Our job as visual analysts is to explore. Our job as data storytellers is to explain.
Exploratory analysis might yield important story points or insights that we can later visualize, but they are not part of the storytelling process. As storytellers, we are focused on explanatory analysis and communicating our discoveries in the form of a story.

The distinction between explanatory and exploratory analysis has an important impact on context, particularly in terms of how we present our results. It is common for people to present exploratory graphics as part of their data story—after all, the discovery process can be a tremendous undertaking, and we are often eager to show off all of our hard work or display every detail we've found! However, going off on this kind of tangent inevitably adds bulk to what should be a streamlined, focused story and muddies the message for the audience.

In addition to telling a story, data storytellers must act as their own editors. This requires trimming unnecessary content away so that the core of the data story remains unencumbered and intact. The following sections cover techniques that help maintain the focus on the story.

recommended reading

For more on visual data discovery and working through exploratory analysis, read my 2016 book, *The Visual Imperative: Creating a Visual Culture of Data Discovery*. Additional resources are provided in Chapter 10.

CONTEXT IN TABLEAU

As you might expect, Tableau provides a number of features to help you incorporate context within your data visualizations. In addition to analytical processes, such as normalizing data, context can be embedded into visualizations by using text elements directly on the canvas. In addition to formatting titles, captions, and legends, Tableau provides two context-saving functions: annotations and tooltips.

ANNOTATIONS

Annotations are extracted information associated with a particular point in a visualization. They are used to call out specific marks, points, or areas in a visualization, and can be accessed by right-clicking on the relevant mark on the canvas. There are three types of annotations (Figure 4.4):

- **Mark:** Select this option to add an annotation that is associated with the selected mark. This option is available only if a data point (mark) is selected.
- **Point:** Select this option to annotate a specific point in the view.
- **Area:** Select this option to annotate an area in the viz, such as a cluster of outliers or a targeted region.

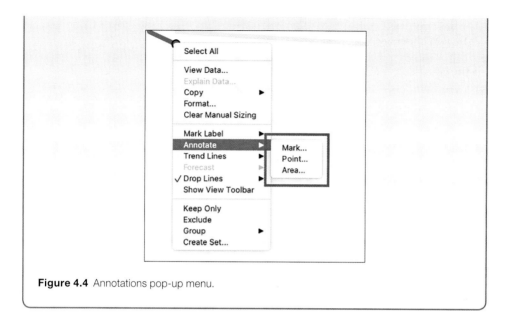

Figure 4.4 Annotations pop-up menu.

TOOLTIPS

The option to add a tooltip can be found on the Marks card (Figure 4.5). Clicking it will create a hover box that displays secondary information when you point at individual marks in the visualization (Figure 4.6). Users can interact with visualizations to learn more by accessing tooltips that include formatted text, dynamic fields in use in the visualization, and even a newer function called Viz-in-Tooltip, in which the tooltip displays a second visualization layer (we'll cover this in a later chapter).

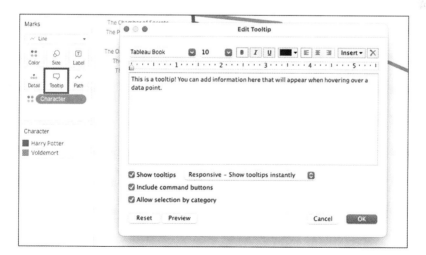

Figure 4.5 Selecting Tooltip from the Marks card provides a dialog box to add other information.

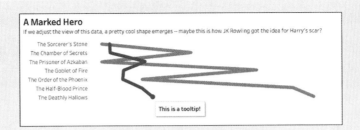

Figure 4.6 Hovering over a mark, when tooltips are activated, is a great way to increase interactivity and layer in additional information.

The Show Me card (Figure 4.7), which you first met in Chapter 3, can guide you in building visualizations that best represent your data. As you choose measures and dimensions and bring them to the shelves, the Show Me card will display which chart types are available based on the fields you've selected. Likewise, if you're unsure of which data to bring over to the shelves, you can use the Show Me card as a tool to select the right measures and dimensions.

Figure 4.7 The Tableau Show Me card, opened on symbol maps.

FILTERING OUT, ZEROING IN

Filters are a great way to help cut out the noise and focus only on the variables or parameters you wish to explore (Figure 4.8). With filters, you can strip out unnecessary information, or you can hone in on specific fields or elements critical to your data story. Like many things in Tableau, filtering can be done in several ways and several places. You explore some of these when working with real datasets later in this book.

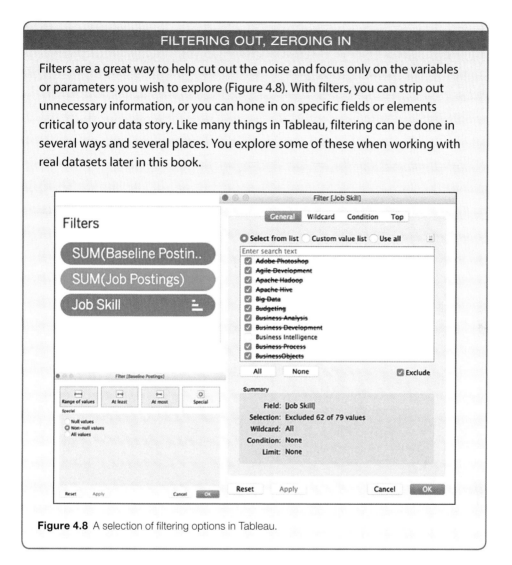

Figure 4.8 A selection of filtering options in Tableau.

Structuring Visual Analytic Stories

Like traditional stories, data stories have shape (and not just bars and bubbles!). This shape is often referred to as the story's "structure." Story structure plays an important role in developing a story's context, and can be broken down into two parts:

- Part 1: Story plot
- Part 2: Story genre

Story Plot

The events of a story (or the main part of a story) form its plot, also called its storyline. These events generally relate to each other in a pattern or a sequence, and the story-teller (or author) is responsible for arranging these actions in a meaningful way to shape the story.

As in other forms of storytelling, the plot of a data story may or may not be organized into a linear sequence (Figure 4.9). Not all data stories are told in order, but they all have one thing in common: They must be true. Data stories are not the place to practice fiction.

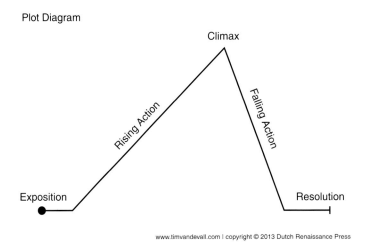

Figure 4.9 The basic plot diagram.

> **note**
>
> The plot diagram is an organizational tool to help map events in a story. Its familiar triangle shape (representing the beginning, middle, and end of a story) was described by Aristotle and later modified by Gustav Freytag, who added rising and falling action to the diagram. Though it was originally designed for traditional stories, data stories can be built using this same framework.

For the purposes of data storytelling, there are eight basic "plots" to help shape your visual data story. Can you identify the plot used in the *Harry Potter* example (Hint: We were telling a story of aggressive acts *over* the series)?

- **Change over time:** See a visual history as told through a simple metric or trend.
- **Drill down:** Start big, and get more and more granular to find meaning.

- **Zoom out:** Reverse the particular, from the individual to a larger group.
- **Contrast:** The "this" or "that."
- **Spread:** Help people see the light and the dark, or reach of data (disbursement).
- **Intersections:** Things that cross over, or progress ("less than" to "more than").
- **Factors:** Things that work together to build up to a higher-level effect.
- **Outliers:** A powerful way to show something outside the realm of normal.

Story Genre

The other half of story structure is its genre. Like the diversity in plot, there is more than one genre to choose from. In fact, there are seven genres of narrative visualization: the magazine style, the annotated chart, the partitioned poster, the flow chart, the comic strip, the slide short, and the conglomerate film/video/animation (Figure 4.10). Developed by Segel and Heer,[3] these genres vary primarily in the number of frames and the ordering of visual elements.

Figure 4.10 Genres of narrative visualization by Segel and Heer.

In Tableau, you can use dashboards and story points in each of these genres, and we will explore how to build them in a later chapter. For now, keep in mind that visual data stories are most effective when they have constrained interactions at various checkpoints and allow the user to explore and engage with the story without veering too far away from the intended narrative. Stories unfold, and each visualization should

---

3. Segel, E.; and Heer, J. "Narrative Visualization: Telling Stories with Data." *IEEE Transactions on Visualization and Computer Graphics* 16, no. 6 (2010): 1139–1148. https://doi.org/10.1109/TVCG.2010.179

highlight one story point at a time (whether within the same visualization or within multiple visualizations) as storytellers layer points to build a complete data narrative.

Audience Analysis for Storytelling

A successful data storyteller has to be an expert in their craft, able to meld the worlds of data visualization and storytelling together into a cohesive whole. However, the story is only half of the equation. A story is a piece of communication, and like every communication, stories are part of a two-way dialogue between the sender (you) and the receiver (your audience). If the story gets interrupted or otherwise lost in translation, you've lost the ability to communicate and will likely fail. Therefore, storytellers need to be clear about exactly who is on the receiving end of their story and to have confidence that they have the information needed to build the right story for their audience.

Many visualization instructors might describe this step of the story-building process in terms of asking the "right" questions, although a lot of ambiguity surrounds just what these questions are. Just as with any type of analysis, there is no silver bullet approach for gathering audience expectations or stakeholder requirements. Questions, like stories, have entropy: They change based on everything from the nature of the relationship of the storyteller to the audience to the action the audience would like to take to the mechanism through which the story is presented. So, a good storyteller knows that the trick isn't asking the *right* questions but rather asking *many* questions. It's okay to be really, really curious, even insatiable in your desire to thoroughly understand your audience and every situation you encounter (curiosity and critical thinking are two "soft skills" at the top of employers' desired skills lists today). Visual analytics are iterative, and building a piece of visual communication, whether it involves a story or something else, is a process of compromise between what you want to say and what the audience needs to hear. Ultimately, you need to be able to learn as much as you can about your audience and what they need to know and then build a story that anticipates and delivers on those audience needs.

Curiosity is a learned skill. It takes time to develop a palate for asking the right research questions and plucking out the relevant details from the noise. Remember, visual data storytelling is fact, not fiction, and as such involves a requisite degree of research as you move through visual analysis. As you practice molding yourself into a thoughtful questioner, however, you can use some of the same journalistic questions that help to parse out the correct context for a story—particularly who, what, why, and how—to make sure you build a presentation that will resonate with your audience and give them the information they need to take action. Let's look more closely at these questions.

Who

Be specific about your audience. Avoid generalizations and assumptions. Taking a broad view of your audience leads to the tendency to overlook nuances and specific needs that might help you zero in on what that audience needs and wants to hear, as well as how you can best communicate with them to capture their interest. Also, narrowing your view of your audience will show you who the decision makers and key influencers are, who needs and wants to hear your story, and whose buy-in you really need to earn. Remember, engaging with your audience is a critical part of successful storytelling.

It's also important to consider the effects of your relationship with the audience when creating your data story. Do they know you? Do they trust you? Do they believe that you are a credible and reliable source of information and insights? The answers to these questions are important because they might influence how you structure your presentation as well as any pre- or post-presentation communication. Your audience must believe in you as an analyst *and* a storyteller before they will listen to your story and be open to taking any actions you might suggest.

What

Analytics begins with understanding data—what you have, what you need, its capabilities and its limitations. Additionally, you should have a realistic view of your data's quality and validity: Those characteristics determine the data's ability to help you answer business questions or explore a hypothesis, and they suggest whether you should seek additional or external data to complete your dataset for analysis. Understanding your data also requires you to have a good grasp of how you might visually represent this data compellingly and accurately, so that you are practicing "no harm" data visualization as you design your narrative.

In addition to knowing the ins and outs of your data, be sure you've asked enough questions to work out what your audience is asking of you, or what story they are asking you to tell with the information you have at your disposal. Aim to have a solid alignment of ideas between which questions can be answered with your data and which insights or information your audience needs or wants; otherwise, your data story will fall flat, unable to satisfy the audience's expectations.

Why

Every good story should prompt an action, whether you are building a story intended to help your audience to make a decision; to cause them to change their opinion; or to convince, persuade, or educate them. Ultimately, you should be crystal clear about your goal in telling the story, and why your audience should care about what you are saying. This understanding helps both to ensure your story is meaningful and necessary and to give you a clear target for building logical arguments toward a salient end goal.

To help crystalize the answers to the "why" part of the equation, be able to articulate clear and concise answers to the following questions:

- Who is your audience? (They might not be as homogenous as you think.)
- What do they want?
- What do they need?
- How might they be feeling?
- What action do they need to take?
- What type of communication do they prefer?
- How well do they know the data?
- What beliefs or bias might they have that you need to reinforce or challenge?
- What, specifically, are you sharing with your audience?
- What, specifically, do you want them to do with this information?

If you cannot readily answer most (if not all) of these questions, you might need to revisit your purpose.

How

Finally, the communication medium and channel you use to present your story matter. In fact, they have a number of implications for how you deliver your story, as well as how much influence you have as a storyteller and how your audience can interact with you as well as with the story itself. Earlier in this chapter, we looked at some options in Tableau for keeping context locked inside a visualization that help support narration. Although there are many facets to explore in this step, one of the most constructive is the differences between data stories delivered as narrated, live versions and those that are non-narrated or otherwise "static" presentations.

Narrated

Narrated storytelling presentations are delivered live—either in person or virtually—and the storyteller has the ability to narrate the presentation and guide the experience. In this mode, the storyteller has full control of the narrative and is able to direct the audience's attention to points of interest and facilitate transitions between story points, explaining any potential areas of ambiguity and emphasizing or softening points as needed.

In addition to the ability to direct the audience, live presenters have an obligation to be sensitive to the audience and respond to their needs. As a presenter, you have a front-row seat from which to view your audience. Remember: You are not a TV screen—you can react and respond to visual cues to determine whether you need to speed up or slow down or go into more or less detail as you move through your presentation. One tip I give to students learning to present is to always have more pieces of the story than you are planning to share stored in your back pocket. That way, if you need to dive into details or add an embellishing point to your story, you can introduce that information without adding junk into your presentation and interfering with the flow of your data story.

Non-Narrated

Non-narrated storytelling presentations are delivered without the benefit of a story-teller to guide the experience, such as reports, emails, and even dashboards. In this case, the storyteller relinquishes control of the audience's experience and relies on the tool used to distribute the information.

To ensure the integrity of the visuals and the story, a highly curated and detailed view of the information is necessary. In the case of Tableau dashboards or story points, this translates into not just well-crafted visualizations, but cohesive, logical storylines and appropriate filters, highlights, and other venues to let the audience explore visuals without degrading the story or the underlying data's integrity. Pay attention to the device form factor, too, as you will need to be aware of how your story is presented across multiple devices (laptop screens, tablets, smartphones, and so on).

TIPS FOR SUCCESS IN PRESENTATIONS

Telling data stories through a live presentation is as much an art as building the story itself. In addition to having skills in data analysis and visualization, such storytellers must be skilled presenters, equipped with the capability to guide the audience through the story and facilitate a shared experience.

Of course, public speaking in any form isn't a prospect that excites many people. As a statistic made humorous by comedian Jerry Seinfeld notes, according to most studies, people's *number one* fear is public speaking; number two is death. Hence Seinfeld's joke: The average person at a funeral would rather be the one in the casket than the one giving the eulogy.

The secret to overcoming presentation anxiety and polishing up your skills as a speaker is a simple one: practice. Practice gives you opportunities to learn your own strengths as well as identify areas to improve, helps you discover and fine-tune your speaking style, and—perhaps most important—is the one and only venue to building confidence earned from experience.

Here are a few tips to help you become more comfortable about going "on stage":

- There's wisdom in the mantra "Practice makes perfect." Rehearse, revise, rehearse.

- Write out speaking points, not speaking paragraphs. Document three to four important points you want to make for each slide to be your compass.

- Design presentations to *support* your story, not presentations to *tell* your story. Your audience should be listening to you, not reading slides. Just as in a chart or graph, maximize the data-to-ink ratio and keep visuals clean and minimal.

Summary

This chapter looked closely at the importance of understanding data's context and its role in helping visual analysts ask the right questions to build a story framework. You learned about exploratory and explanatory analysis and strategies for successful storytelling, including narrative flow, considerations for spoken versus written narratives that support visuals, and structures that can support stories for maximum impact.

The next chapter looks at the importance of choosing the right visual—or combinations of visuals—to support your data story, as well as how to build fundamental visualizations in Tableau.

CHAPTER 5

FUNDAMENTAL DATA VISUALIZATIONS

This chapter introduces the types of charts and graphs most commonly used to visually communicate data. We discuss appropriate use cases for each and get hands-on to create examples from the catalog of charts available in Tableau. You will learn techniques to help you assess when to use fundamental data visualizations and how to generate them according to best practices, as well as helpful considerations for when to avoid certain types of charts. We'll also explore some of the special features available in Tableau to help you get the most from your visuals.

When it comes to visually representing data insights, there is no shortage of charts and graphs to choose from. From traditional graphs to innovative hand-coded visualizations, a continuum of visualizations exists to translate data into meaning using shapes, color, and other visual cues. However, each visualization type is intended to represent different types of data in specific ways so as to best showcase its insights. In this chapter, we'll look at the some of the widely used visualization types available on the Tableau Show Me card (Figure 5.1) to help you choose the right type of chart for your data. We'll look at maps separately in the next chapter.

Figure 5.1 The Show Me card shows the fundamental types of visualizations available in Tableau. The thumbnails on the card become "activated" when there is data on the canvas required to build each type, and a prompt below each thumbnail helps analysts to identify which types of measures and dimensions are needed to create each viz.

> **note**
>
> All visualizations created in this chapter were made using real datasets that are included in Tableau's library of sample datasets available at https://public.tableau.com/app/resources/sample-data. Additionally, datasets are provided via the companion website for this text. We'll primarily use the "Netflix Movies and TV" dataset. I encourage you to download the data so that you can follow along with the step-by-step tutorials to create each of the visualizations discussed in this chapter.

The Bar Chart

A traditional favorite, the bar chart is one of the most common ways to visualize data. It is best suited for numerical data that can be divided into distinct categories to compare information and reveal trends at a glance (Figure 5.2).

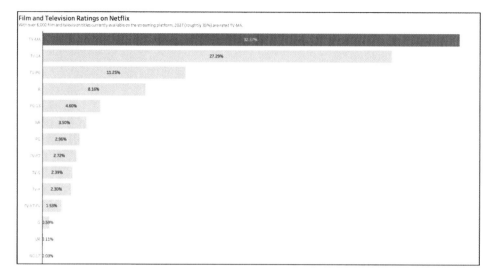

Figure 5.2 This simple, classic bar chart with highlight color shows the percentage of film ratings across available Netflix film and television titles. For a full look at the formatting of this visualization, see Figure 5.8.

Here are a few ways to spice up the classic bar chart:

- Bars can be oriented on the vertical or horizontal axis, which can be helpful for spotting trends.
- Additional layers of information can be added by using clustered bars or by stacking related data.
- Color can be added for more impact or to overlay for immediate insight.
- Trend lines and other annotations can be added to highlight important data points.
- Use side-by-side or stacked bars (Figure 5.3) to give depth to your analysis and answer multiple questions at once. Bar-in-bar charts—another useful option that resolves some qualitative challenges associated particularly with stacked bar charts—are explored in a later chapter.
- Bar charts can be combined with maps or line charts to act as filters that correspond to different data points as they are selected.
- Multiple bar charts could be set on a dashboard to help viewers quickly compare information without navigating several charts.

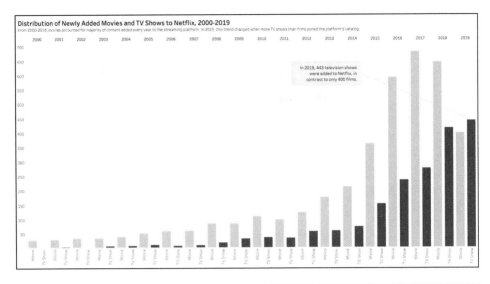

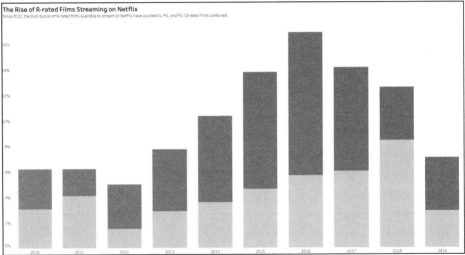

Figure 5.3 Alternative bar charts: A side-by-side bar chart with highlight color, banded columns, and annotation, and a stacked bar chart with an alert color.

Tableau How-To: Bar Chart

To begin creating a vertical bar chart in Tableau, place a dimension on the Rows shelf and a measure on the Columns shelf; to create a horizontal bar chart, place a measure on the Rows shelf and a dimension on the Columns shelf (Figure 5.4). You will notice that the Bar mark type is already selected on the Mark card. Tableau automatically selects this mark type when the data view matches one of the two field arrangements mentioned previously.

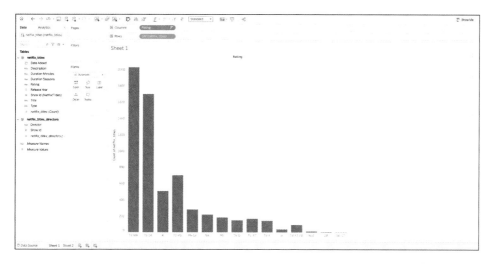

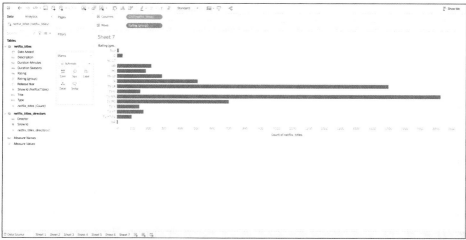

Figure 5.4 Bar charts can be oriented either vertically (top) or horizontally (bottom).

tip

Instead of manually rearranging pills on the shelves, you can use the Swap Rows and Columns button on the toolbar to rearrange rows and columns and toggle between views (Figure 5.5).

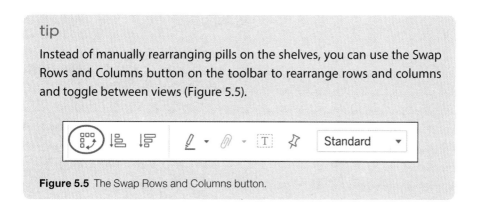

Figure 5.5 The Swap Rows and Columns button.

The process of creating a bar chart presents an excellent opportunity to talk about the importance of sorting. This step is especially relevant when developing bar charts and other parts-of-whole visualizations.

Sorting Data in Tableau

There are many ways to sort data in Tableau, depending on the type of visualization you are working with, or the area of the viz you are formatting. When viewing a visualization, data can be sorted using single-click options from an axis, header, or field label. Additional sorting options include sorting manually in headers and legends, using the toolbar sort icons, and sorting from the Sort menu.

In bar charts, it is best practice to sort your data in either ascending or descending order, depending on the use case. An easy way to do this is to use the corresponding Sort icons on the toolbar (Figure 5.6).

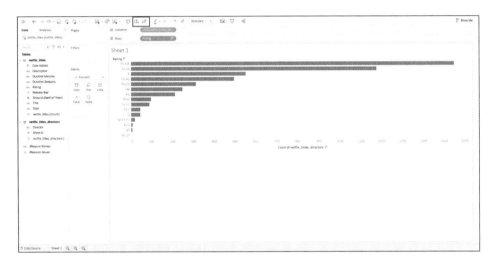

Figure 5.6 Sort icons on the Tableau toolbar enable you to organize your data in ascending or descending order with one click.

It's also important to pay attention to how many bars you have on a horizontal bar chart to avoid the moiré effect (pronounced "mwa-ray"), a type of visual interference that can create a "shimmer" when too many bars are grouped too closely together (Figure 5.7). To reduce the moiré effect, considering limiting your visualization to a "top 10" or equivalent arrangement, or use highlight or alerting colors to reduce visual clutter.

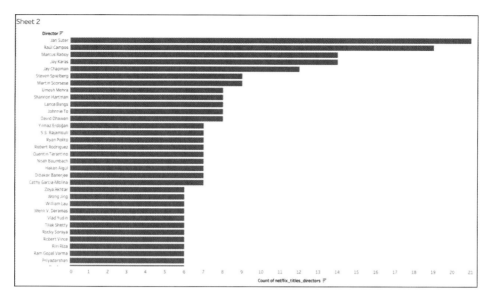

Figure 5.7 Whether vertical or horizontal, too many bars in a bar chart can result in a moiré effect, a visual illusion in which the bars appear to shimmer.

Once you have your bars on the canvas, you can add additional fields to these shelves and further modify your bar chart as desired. For example, you can adjust the color, axis and field labels, annotations, titles, and more (Figure 5.8).

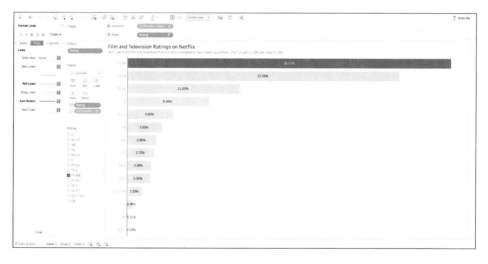

Figure 5.8 A few additional curating steps can help the data presented in this bar chart shine.

The Line Chart

Like the bar chart, the line chart (or time series chart) is one of the most frequently used visualization types. These charts connect individual numeric data points to visualize a sequence of values. As such, they are most commonly used when an element of time is present—hence their alternative title. In fact, the best use case for line charts involves displaying trends over a period of time (Figure 5.9), when your data are ordered, or when interpolation makes sense.

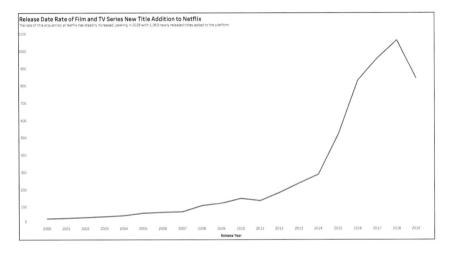

Figure 5.9 This line chart shows film and television title adaptions, by release date, at Netflix from 2000 to 2019.

Dual-axis line charts can be created by bringing two measures to the Rows shelf, and then right-clicking on the second measure and selecting Dual-axis from the drop-down menu. You'll also need to synchronize the axes to ensure that the data is not skewed. Our Netflix dataset does not include the appropriate data to generate a proper dual axis, but you can see an example of a dual-axis line chart in Figure 5.10.

We can accomplish the same effect by breaking down measures on a line chart to see variables independently of one another, using color to distinguish data, as in Figure 5.11. Notice that this method allows us to slice and dice our data, yielding additional insights missed in the combined visualization of Figure 5.9.

Figure 5.10 Create a dual-axis line chart by combining two measures. This produces a line chart with multiple lines.

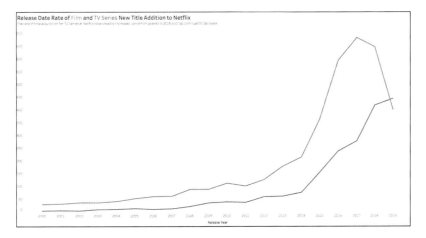

Figure 5.11 Adding multiple layers to a visualization allows you to slice and dice data to derive additional insights that may be hidden in the aggregated data.

tip

Figure 5.11 makes use of clever color-encoding in the visualization title, which eliminates the need to include a color legend that will take up valuable real estate on the visualization.

When two or more lines are present, you can transform line charts by adding additional chart types to deepen the insights. For example, a line chart can be combined with a bar chart (Figure 5.12) to provide visual cues for further investigation. Alternatively, the area under lines can be shaded by filling the space under each respective line; the resulting area chart can extend the analysis and illuminate each line's relative contribution to the whole. Trend lines, such as linear regression and forecasting, can be added to offer even more insights.

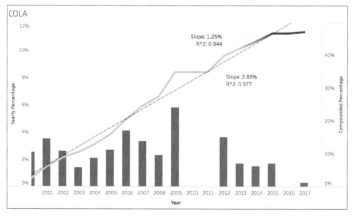

Figure 5.12 Adjust the Marks card to help you combine chart types. This work-in-progress line chart has been combined with a bar chart. It also includes annotations, trend lines, and a color gradient shade element on the line to enhance insight.

Tableau How-To: Line Chart

You create a line chart in Tableau by placing one or more measures on either the Columns shelf or the Rows shelf, and then plotting the measures against either a date or continuous dimension (Figure 5.13). Additionally, the Automatic Marks card drop-down menu will select Line as the mark type. You can further expand line charts by including summary analytics, such as forecasting. Be sure to synchronize or adjust axes to keep the numbers in context.

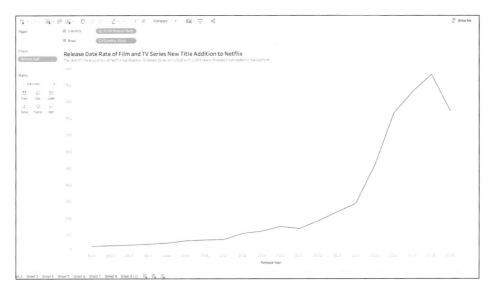

Figure 5.13 With minimal clicks, you can create a simple yet effective time series visualization.

Pie and Doughnut Charts

We all love to hate "dessert charts," particularly the pie chart and its cousin the doughnut. While there are a lot of opinions about why dessert charts make for poor analytic tools, it's more effective to point out the substantial amount of empirical research that provides concrete, evidence-based reasons not to use these charts, as well as the research that has established best practices for when we simply must use them.

While circular charts are not new (Florence Nightingale's 1858 Coxcomb plot serves as a prime example), and many do offer strong impact in terms of storytelling, the truth is that humans are just not very good at reading and understanding angles. Further, the many distortion effects caused by too many slices (which occur with both pie and doughnut charts) create additional comprehension issues that diminish pie charts' likelihood of being considered useful analytic visualization. Even so, these charts remain among the most misused and overused of chart types. Nevertheless, with a few tweaks, both of these notorious chart types can be used, with discretion, as viable options to visualize parts of a whole, or percentages.

In both types of charts, the circle represents the 100% whole, and the size of each wedge (or slice) represents a percentage. The trick to properly reading pie or dough-nut charts is to not rely on the angle, but rather to look at area or arc length. To avoid a bad pie chart, focus on comparing only a few values (fewer than six is preferable, and two is best, if possible) and use distinct color separation (or borders or white space) for maximum readability. Doughnut charts can help clarify your data story by including a key takeaway in the center white space (Figure 5.14).

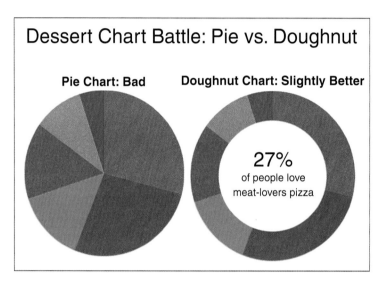

Figure 5.14 A side-by-side comparison of an unlabeled pie chart and a doughnut chart displaying percentages of America's favorite pizza toppings.

The first rule of dessert charts is similar to the first rule of *Fight Club*: Don't use dessert charts. Other visualization types—including bar charts and tree maps—are typically better suited to showcase the information contained within a pie or doughnut chart. However, if you must use a dessert chart, consider the following points:

- Make sure all wedges add up to 100%.
- "Slice" as few values as possible—ideally two, but up to five is appropriate.
- Start at noon and move clockwise to "sort" slices from largest to smallest value.
- Add labels to quantify the exact wedge value.
- Avoid 3D (i.e., three-dimensional effects)! While this is a practice to keep in mind for all data visualizations (the exception being certain types of topographical and

related data that is beyond the scope of this book), it is especially imperative (and detrimental) in dessert charts, where our ability to read arcs and angles is already severely reduced.

- Use color and white space to keep wedges clearly distinguishable.
- When possible, elevate a pie chart to a doughnut chart, and utilize the "doughnut hole" to include a key metric or key performance indicator (KPI).

We'll employ these practices in the next hands-on example.

> **note**
>
> These pie and doughnut chart visualizations were created using a tiny dataset on pizza toppings that is available on the companion website for this text.

Tableau How-To: Pie and Doughnut Charts

To begin either a pie or doughnut chart, you start by building a basic bar chart or by creating a pie chart directly in the Marks card. This will produce a rather small pie chart from which you can continue to refine and expand the visualization.

> **tip**
>
> You can increase the size by holding down Ctrl+Shift (or holding down Command+Shift on a Mac) and pressing B several times. You can also change your view to Entire View to automatically resize the viz.

Although we could build a dessert chart by using either of these methods or by working directly from the Show Me card, I recommend beginning with a basic bar chart. With this approach, it can be an easy walk-back if you decide to err on the side of a more accessible visualization.

Begin by building a basic bar chart and then use the Show Me card to select the pie chart option (Figure 5.15). You'll note that the Marks card has likewise changed from automatic (or bar) to pie.

Figure 5.15 Begin building a pie or doughnut chart by starting with a basic bar chart, then selecting the pie chart option from the Show Me card.

note

To keep this data visualization aligned with best practices, I've filtered down to movies only, then further narrowed the data to show only the four rating categories most commonly associated with films (G, PG, PG-13, and R).

Before we go on, enlarge your pie chart to a more appropriate size. Next, sort your wedges by first using the Sort option on the Color Marks card menu, then sorting by Field and descending (Figure 5.16).

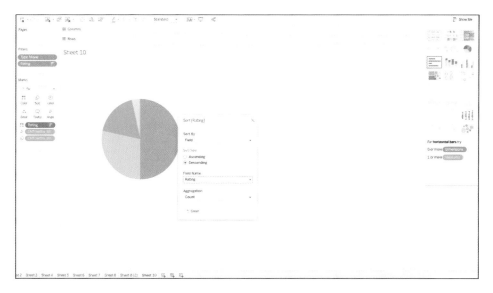

Figure 5.16 A few quick steps can help ensure the pie chart aligns to best practices.

From here, we could further refine this basic pie chart by sorting, adjusting color, and so forth. However, while there is no one-click or Show Me option to change a pie chart into a doughnut chart, a few additional steps will transform your view:

1. First, we must duplicate the pie chart. This is achieved by creating a fake axis on our Rows/Columns shelves. Double-click in the Rows shelf to type there; then input a 1. This will create a SUM(1) field. From here, click on the newly formed pill's drop-down menu and change the measure from Sum to Minimum.

2. Duplicate this pill by either performing the same exercise again in the Rows shelf, or by using your mouse to drag-and-drop duplicate the field using the Command key.

3. Now that we have two identical pie charts, we will essentially use the second pie as the middle part of the doughnut. On the second MIN mark on your Marks card, remove any fields from Color (this should render the viz gray). If the Size marks card includes any pills, remove them, and then reduce the size by roughly half. When finished, your canvas should look similar to Figure 5.17.

4. Right-click the second instance of MIN pill on the Columns shelf and select Dual Axis. This will allow the two charts to lay on top of each other (Figure 5.18).

5. From here, we need to begin formatting the doughnut chart. First, right-click the top axis to synchronize the axes. We can clean the view by further removing axis headers.

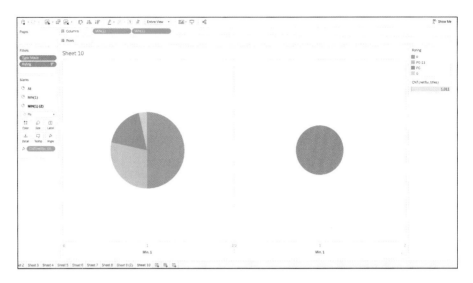

Figure 5.17 Transform a pie chart into a doughnut chart by first duplicating the pie chart and then manually adjusting the color and size.

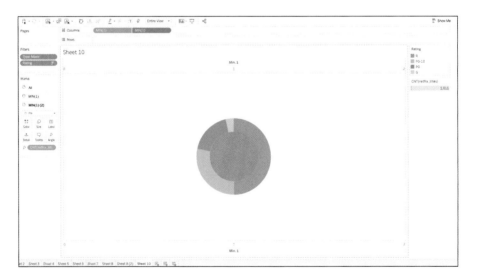

Figure 5.18 By using the dual axis function, we begin to layer our two pies to form an early doughnut chart.

6. On the Marks card for the second pie, change the color to gray, and bring any value you'd like to display in the doughnut hole onto the Labels card (you can also experiment with more customized text-box additions to fill this space by using the doughnut chart in a dashboard, which we'll cover in a later chapter).

After a little bit of curation, your final pie chart should resemble that shown in Figure 5.19.

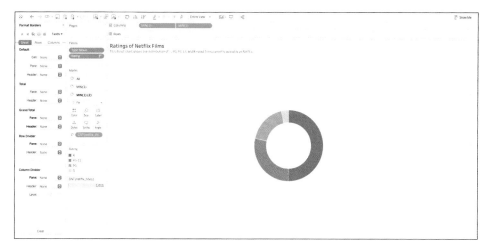

Figure 5.19 A complete doughnut chart with additional color work and worksheet formatting.

SKETCHING YOUR STORY

Sketching ideas for your graphics can facilitate the artistic process of storyboarding the output of your visual analysis (Figure 5.20). If you can create a vision of your story, you can use it as a guide to curate meaningful charts and graphs. While Tableau doesn't support sketching, these guides can be helpful as you work to curate your visual in Tableau to tell its best story.

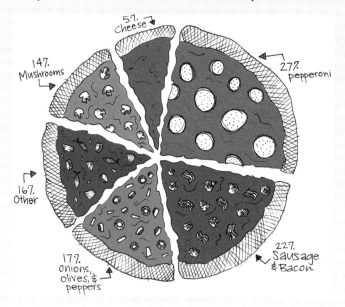

Figure 5.20 Sketching stories can facilitate the artistic process of visualization and help you see your end goal as you work to curate it in Tableau.

The Scatter Plot

Scatter plots are an effective way to visualize numerical variables to compare and quickly identify patterns, trends, concentrations (clusters), and outliers. These charts can give audiences a sense of where to focus discovery efforts further and are best used to investigate relationships between numerical variables. Scatter plots are particularly useful when exploring statistical relationships such as linear regression. Figure 5.21 provides an example of the scatter plot.

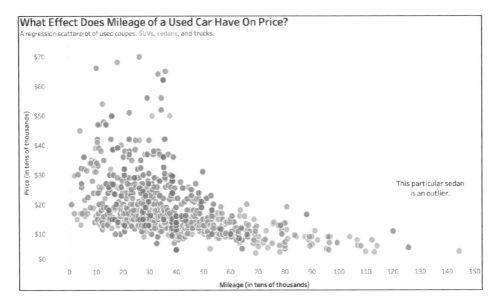

Figure 5.21 Scatter plot example.

Tableau How-To: Scatter Plots

You can create a scatter plot in Tableau in two ways: as a **simple scatter plot** or a **matrix scatter plot**.

You create simple scatter plots by dragging a measure to the Columns shelf and a measure to the Rows shelf. When you plot one number against another, the result is a Cartesian chart—a one-mark scatter plot with a single *x, y* coordinate (Figure 5.22).

To view all of your measures, deselect the Aggregate Measures option from the Analysis menu (Figure 5.23).

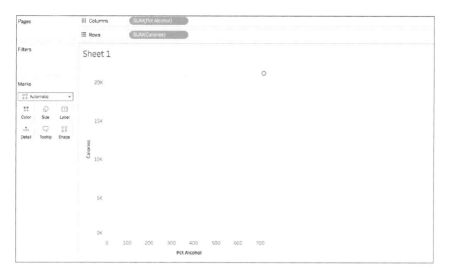

Figure 5.22 Simple scatter plots begin with aggregated measures, showing only one mark.

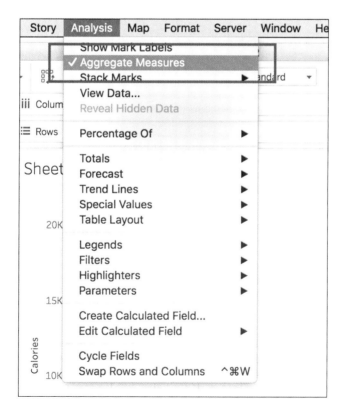

Figure 5.23 Deselect Aggregate Measures to view all of your data points on a scatter plot.

Doing so generates a simple scatter plot, as shown in Figure 5.24.

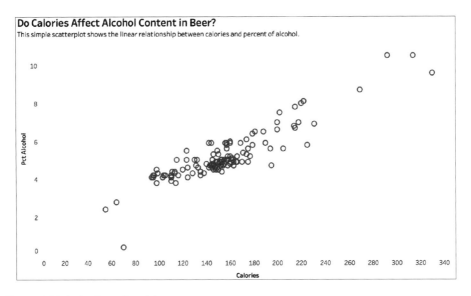

Figure 5.24 A simple scatter plot.

You can add depth and visual richness to a scatterplot in the following ways:

- Bring over dimensions from the Data pane onto the Marks card and use them to add color or additional shapes onto the scatter plot.

- Change the shape of the data via the Marks card to provide additional relevance and visual cues. You can choose these shapes from a set of sample default shapes as well as a selection of shape palettes included in Tableau (Figure 5.25). You can also consider custom shapes, which we'll discuss in a later chapter.

- Incorporate filters to reduce noise and help limit the investigation to the factors that matter most to your analysis.

Scatter plots are excellent candidates to include statistical information for the purpose of reviewing trends and other analytics. Via Tableau's Analytics pane, you can add a variety of analytic models to highlight the statistics in your data. Hover the cursor over the trend lines to display statistical information used to create the line(s), as shown in Figure 5.26.

If these shelves contain both dimensions and measures, Tableau will create a **matrix of scatter plots** and place the measures as the innermost fields. Thus, these measures are always to the right of any dimensions that you have also placed on the shelves. The word *innermost* in this case refers to the table structure (Figure 5.27).

Figure 5.25 Choose shapes from the Marks card to add depth to your scatter plot.

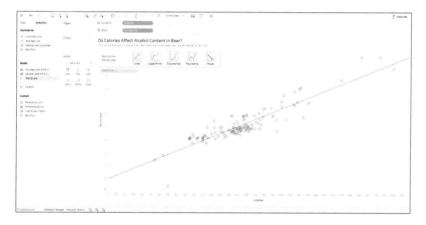

Figure 5.26 A scatter plot with a trend line and summary statistics.

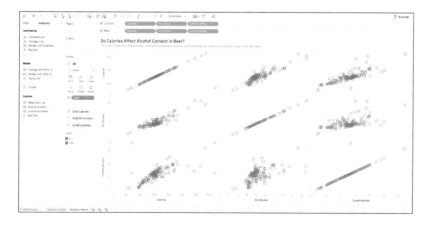

Figure 5.27 A matrix scatter plot.

The Packed Bubble Chart

The bubble chart is a variation of the scatter plot that replaces data points with a cluster of circles (or bubbles), a technique that further emphasizes data that would be rendered on a pie chart, scatter plot, or map. This method shows relational values without regard to axes and is used to display three dimensions of data: two dimensions through the bubble's location and a third dimension through size.

These charts allow for the comparison of entities in terms of their relative positions with respect to each numeric axis and size. The sizes of the bubbles provide details about the data, and colors can be used as an additional encoding cue to answer many questions about the data at once (Figure 5.28). As a technique for adding richness to bubble charts, consider overlaying them on a map to put geographic data quickly into context. Proper labels and annotations can also ensure valuable quantitative information stays firmly contextualized within the visualization.

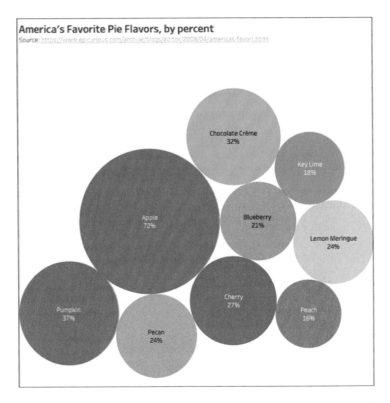

Figure 5.28 A packed bubble chart displays data in a cluster of circles, using size and color to encode the bubbles with meaning.

note

This bubble chart visualization was created using a tiny dataset on America's favorite pie flavors collected by the Epicurious food blog in 2008. The data can be found here: www.epicurious.com/archive/blogs/editor/2008/04/ americas-favori.html. A small, re-creatable table is also shown in Figure 5.29. Note that this data was collected via a "check all that apply" approach, so the total percentage does not equal 100%.

America's Favorite Pie Flavors, by percent
Source: https://www.epicurious.com/archive/blogs/editor/2008/04/americas-favori.html

Pie	
Apple	72
Blueberry	21
Cherry	27
Chocolate Crème	32
Key Lime	18
Lemon Meringue	24
Peach	16
Pecan	24
Pumpkin	37

Figure 5.29 A simple data table showing America's favorite pie flavors as of 2008.

Tableau How-To: Packed Bubble Charts

To create a basic packed bubble chart, drag a dimension to the Columns shelf and a measure to the Rows shelf. Tableau will aggregate the measure as a sum and create a vertical axis to display a bar chart. This is the default functionality when you select one measure and dimension in this manner. Next, use the Show Me card to select the Packed Bubble chart from the list of options (Figure 5.30).

In this example, the size of the bubble represents the number of survey responses, whereas the color of the bubble represents the flavor or pie chosen. The circle is also labeled with the flavor.

As with most chart types, there are ways to add more insights and quantitative context into a packed bubble chart or embellish the chart with storytelling techniques. For example, you can use different dimensions to encode color or adjust labels to add more information (Figure 5.31).

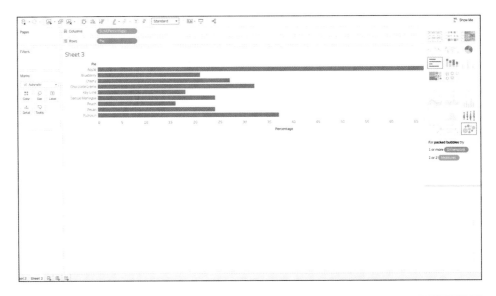

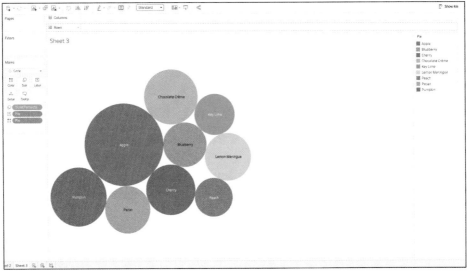

Figure 5.30 Building a packed bubble chart in Tableau begins with building a bar chart and changing the chart type.

Shapes, especially circles, also provide an interesting opportunity to move beyond data visualization tools to bring your story to life in creative ways (assuming, of course, this works for your audience and your story). In Figure 5.32, images of the pie flavors overlay the bubbles, presenting the same data in a more visual way. Because we are interested in the story here more than the analytics, this works.

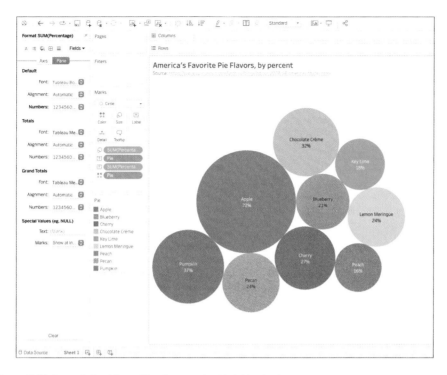

Figure 5.31 In-worksheet formatting for a packed bubble chart.

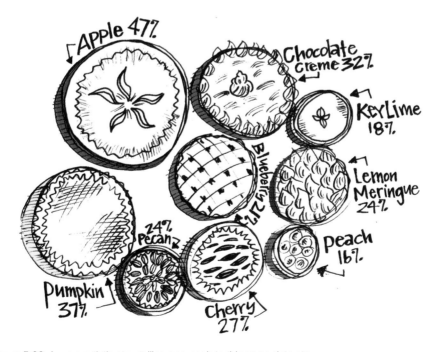

Figure 5.32 A more artistic storytelling approach to this same data story.

> **note**
>
> You might recognize this image from Wake's Pis: A Kid's Guide to Delicious Data Stories. For more of Wake's work, check out www.tableau.com/about/blog/2016/6/viz-long-and-prosper-how-one-young-trekkie-telling-stories-his-data-55767.

The Tree Map

One of the more advanced visualizations covered in this chapter, the tree map uses a series of rectangles of various sizes to show relative proportions (Figure 5.33). It works especially well if the data being visualized has a hierarchical structure (with parent nodes, children, and so on) or when analyzing a parts-to-whole relationship with more divisions than are suitable for a pie chart. As its name suggests, a tree map divides and subdivides based on parts of a whole by breaking down into smaller rectangles nested within a larger rectangle, often of a different color or different color gradient, to emphasize its relationship to the larger whole.

Figure 5.33 This tree map illustrates data (obtained through a survey) on students' perceptions of how schools should fight back against cyberbullying. The sizes and shapes of the rectangles give further details about their relationships within the hierarchy of total answers.

The tree map also provides a much more efficient way to see this relationship when working with large amounts of data by making efficient use of space. It is ideal for legibly showing hundreds (or perhaps even thousands) of items simultaneously within a single visualization.

Tableau How-To: Tree Maps

Use dimensions to define the structure of a tree map and measures to define the size (or color) of the rectangles.

The process of building a tree map in Tableau begins similarly to building a packed bubble chart: by creating a basic bar chart. Drag a dimension to the Columns shelf and a measure to the Rows shelf. Tableau will aggregate the measure as a sum and create a vertical axis to display a bar chart (Figure 5.34). From here, use the Show Me card to select a tree map from the list of available chart types.

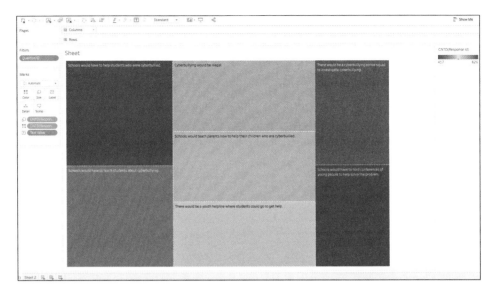

Figure 5.34 Building a tree map in Tableau begins with building a bar chart and changing the chart type.

In this example, we are using survey data to create the tree map and examine how many respondents selected each of the options presented. Both the size of the rectangles and their color are determined by the value of Response ID—the greater the sum of unique responses for each category, the darker and larger its box (this is further clarified by the color legend at right). Although this dataset does not include any "negative" values, Tableau has automatically selected a diverging color palette, rather than a sequential palette. Here, it is useful to quickly identify the top responses from the lowest by using visual color cues.

Size and color are crucial elements in tree maps. You can modify a tree map by adjusting how color is utilized. For example, in Figure 5.35, the count of Response ID has been removed from the Color shelf and replaced with Grade (6–12); now, rather than seeing total responses, we can review the responses by grade level to see how student opinions differ by age. In the revised tree map, Grade determines the color of the rectangles and the count of Responses still determines the size of rectangles, allowing us to see top responses per grade. This refinement of the view would help cyberbullying researchers identify which responses may be most appropriate by grade level.

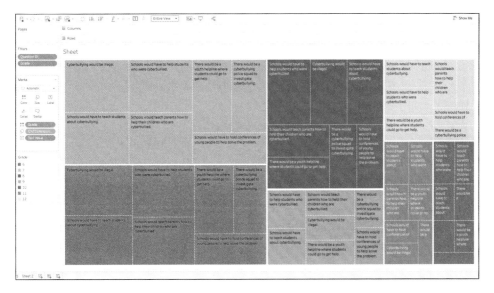

Figure 5.35 Modify elements on the Marks card to adjust the elements of color and shape in a tree map.

The Heat Map

A heat map graph is a great way to compare categorical data using color (Figure 5.36). Similar to the tree map, a heat map depicts the values for a variable as a hierarchy. It is similar in concept to the type of complex visual data representation that the meteorologist on your local weather forecast might use to illustrate rainfall patterns across a region. However, creating hierarchies within Tableau is not limited to use with maps, and hierarchies can be a useful function for other drill-down activities.

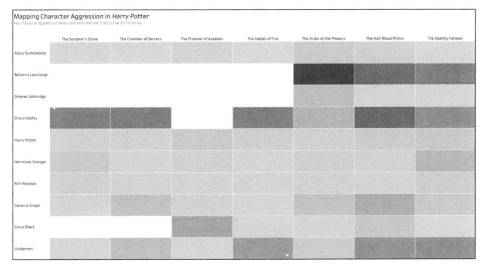

Figure 5.36 A heat map of frequency of aggressive acts committed in Harry Potter.

Here are some tips for tailoring this type of visualization to your audience:

- Add a size variation for squares to show the concentration of intersecting factors while adding a third element.

- Use a shape other than a square to convey meaning in a more impactful way.

> **note**
>
> The heat map visualizations in this chapter were created from a large, collected dataset on character aggression in the *Harry Potter* series, the culmination of which was presented at the 2017 Harry Potter Academic Conference hosted by Chestnut Hill University. The full dataset is available at the companion website for this text.

Tableau How-To: Heat Maps

Building a heat map in Tableau takes a few more clicks than with some of the other charts discussed (Figure 5.37):

- Place one (or more) dimensions onto the Columns shelf *and* one (or more) dimensions on the Rows shelf.

- Select Square as the mark type on the Marks card.

- Place a measure on the Color shelf.

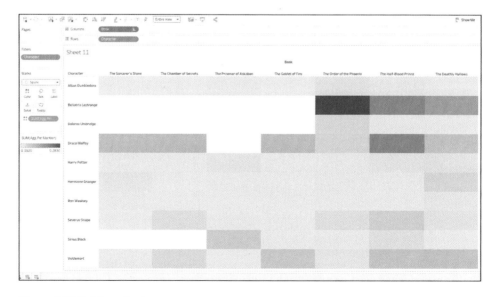

Figure 5.37 Building a heat map.

> note
>
> Since this is quite a large dataset, in Figure 5.37 I have already manually sorted the order of books (you can see the Sort icon on the Book pill) and filtered the number of characters (you can see the Name pill in on the Filters shelf).

There are a few more steps to curate this heat map. The preceding example uses the default blue gradient color palette. However, other color palettes might be more appropriate, depending on your data. For example, Figure 5.35 shows the use of a red-gold gradient scheme to progressively darken the cell color in line with characters' aggressive action counts. You can access the Colors box in the Marks card, and then select Edit Colors to open the Edit Colors dialog box (Figure 5.38). From here you can select another color palette from the drop-down menu—either a gradient palette or a diverging palette.

- If you **select** the Use Full Color Range check box for a diverging option, Tableau will assign the starting number a full intensity and the ending number a full intensity.

- If you **don't select** the Use Full Color Range check box, Tableau will automatically assign the color intensity as if the range were from −100 to +100, maximizing the color contrast as much as possible.

Figure 5.38 Use the Edit Colors dialog box to select an appropriate color scheme for a heat map.

Additional visual cues, such as lines, are also important contributors to curating heat maps. You can add borders to each colored cell in the view by revisiting the Color Editor box and selecting an appropriate border color from the Effects portion of the border dialog box as you further refine your final visualization (Figure 5.39).

Figure 5.39 Adding borders to colored cells helps to distinguish individual cells in the view.

RECOMMENDED READING

Check out the Tableau white paper *Which Chart or Graph* for additional information: www.tableau.com/learn/whitepapers/which-chart-or-graph-is-right-for-you.

This chapter's discussion covers the majority of fundamental data visualization types shown on the Tableau Show Me card. In the next chapter, we'll take a look at one more visualization type: maps.

Summary

These exercises have walked us through most, but not all, of the visualization types available natively on the Tableau Show Me card. There are still two more important visualization types to discuss. We'll cover two types of fundamental maps in the next chapter.

CHAPTER 6

FUNDAMENTAL MAPS

As a continuation of the previous chapter, this chapter introduces two fundamental types of maps available on the Tableau Show Me card: proportional symbol and choropleth (or filled) maps (Figure 6.1). Again, we'll discuss appropriate use cases for each and get hands-on to create examples in Tableau. We'll also see how to generate these maps according to best practices, and consider some helpful guidelines specifically for mapping data.

Figure 6.1 The Tableau Show Me card offers two fundamental map types.

> **note**
>
> All visualizations created in this chapter were created using a Centers for Disease Control and Prevention (CDC) collected dataset on Lyme disease case counts by county from 2000 to 2015. This Lyme disease dataset is publicly available from the CDC at www.cdc.gov/lyme/stats/index.html.

If you want to analyze or present your data geographically, Tableau has several native mapping capabilities. Maps can be used to display geographic data or to communicate answers to spatial questions, such as "Which states offer the most analytics education programs?" or "Which regions in the United States have the most cases of Lyme disease?"

While maps can be a great way to tell a story about your data, remember that they are a type of visualization and do have an appropriate use case. Depending on the question you are trying to answer or the insight you are trying to communicate, another chart type might be a more appropriate fit. Before you begin building a map, take a careful look at your data, your analysis, and your story. Maps, as Tableau explains, should answer questions with both an *appropriate* data representation and an *attractive* data representation. As a storytelling device, maps can be particularly tricky in their tendency to mislead or inadvertently cause people to misinterpret the data or to dictate a not-quite-true story.

Tableau can be customized to create several types of maps. This section covers the two most commonly used types: proportional symbol maps and choropleth (or filled) maps.

> note
>
> Tableau capabilities include many advanced map types and customization functions that are not covered in this text. Tutorials and use case information for more advanced maps—for example, point distribution maps, which help you look for visual clusters of data; flow (or path) maps, which connect paths to see where something went (e.g., storms or product sales) over time; and spider (or origin-destination) maps, which show how an origin location and one or more destination locations interact—can be found online. For more info, visit https://help.tableau.com/current/pro/desktop/en-us/maps_build.htm.

WHAT GEODATA DOES TABLEAU SUPPORT?

Tableau recognizes a set of geographic roles defined by a geocoding database that uses latitude and longitude coordinates. By default, Tableau supports the following kinds of geodata, among others:

- Worldwide airport codes

- Cities

- Countries/regions/territories

- States/provinces

- Some postal codes and second-level administrative districts (county-equivalents)

- U.S. area codes

- Core-Based Statistical Areas (CBSA)

- Metropolitan Statistical Areas (MSA)

- Congressional districts

- Zip codes

Additionally, Tableau organizes geographic roles within a hierarchical order. The order is City > County > Zip Code > CBSA/MSA > Area Code > State > Country/Region. When you place multiple geographic fields on the Detail list on the Marks card, Tableau plots the data points in the field with the highest geographic role on this list.

Connecting to Geographic Data

Although you are already familiar with connecting to data in Tableau at this point, geographic data comes in many shapes and formats. For this reason, it is useful to walk through this step of the process again within the context of mapping and discuss where geodata nuances might affect the process as you prepare to work with geographic data.

> **note**
>
> Newer visions of Tableau Desktop can connect directly to spatial files (such as shapefiles and geoJSON files). However, following the precedent established in this book, the examples in this chapter demonstrate connecting to data in Excel.

In this exercise, we'll connect to a dataset of cases of Lyme disease. This dataset provides a count of Lyme disease cases by state and county from 2000 to 2015. You'll notice that this data is so well prepared that the Data Interpreter option does not appear (Figure 6.2).

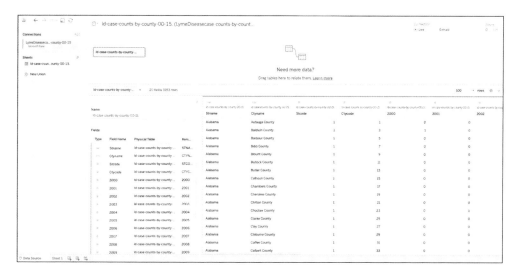

Figure 6.2 This dataset, available from the CDC, contains the number of cases of Lyme disease over a 15-year period.

Assigning Geographic Roles

After connecting to your data source, you might need to take a few more steps before your geographic data is fully prepared for analysis in Tableau. These steps will not always be necessary to create a map and might differ depending on your data and the type of map you intend to create. In almost all cases, geographic fields should have a data type of string, have a data role of dimension, and be assigned the appropriate geographic roles. There is one exception: Latitude/longitude should have a data type of number (decimal), have a data role of measure, and be assigned the Latitude and Longitude geographic roles.

Let's practice adjusting data types for geographic data in the CDC dataset. This simple dataset has two geographic fields: State and County. Tableau has correctly identified these data types as string; however, clicking on the field and looking at the geographic roles reveals that none has been assigned (Figure 6.3). You might need to assign or edit the geographic role assigned by Tableau. In this example, two things must be done:

- Adjust the State field to the geographic role of State
- Adjust the County field to the geographic role of County

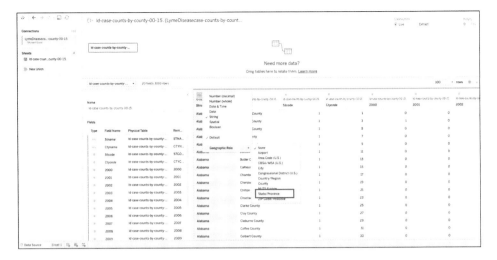

Figure 6.3 Geographic roles can be assigned or changed directly from the data source screen. They can also be changed in a worksheet.

After you make this adjustment, the data type icon will change to a globe, indicating that the field now has a geographic role assigned (Figure 6.4). Further, the icon designated in blue indicates that Tableau has assigned this field as a dimension. This is correct.

⊕ ld-case-counts-by-county-00-15.	⊕ ld-case-counts-by-county-00-15.
Stname	**Ctyname**
Alabama	Autauga County
Alabama	Baldwin County
Alabama	Barbour County
Alabama	Bibb County
Alabama	Blount County
Alabama	Bullock County
Alabama	Butler County

Figure 6.4 The globe icon reflects the geodata field assignment in Tableau.

As one more data preparation step, notice that the field for County Name includes both the name of the county and the word "County." This extra information will disable Tableau from recognizing the county names, but it provides a great opportunity to use the "split" feature available when right-clicking this data field (Figure 6.5).

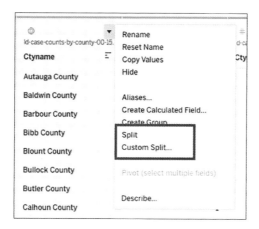

Figure 6.5 Data can be "split" in the preparation process using the split feature.

Since we need to split the data using a consistent space between the county name and the word "County," we can simply use Split. For the sake of illustration, we can also choose Custom Split, which enables you to input the separator as well as the desired number of splits (Figure 6.6). Note that for this function to work as expected, all separators must be consistent.

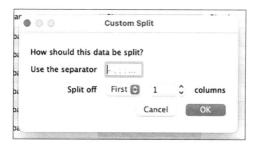

Figure 6.6 For custom splits, choose the separator and split off as desired.

Splitting the data will result in two new columns at the end of the dataset. For clarity's sake, hide your original column, then rename and verify your data type and the geographic roles of the new columns. Since this is data we've effectively created within Tableau, you'll see an = in front of the new column, similar to newly created calculated fields on the Data pane (Figure 6.7).

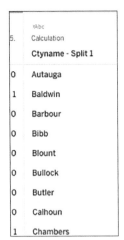

Figure 6.7 Splitting data results in new columns that should be reviewed to ensure they are properly prepared for analysis.

When you assign the correct geographic role to a field in Tableau, the software will also assign a latitude and longitude to each location. It does so by finding a match that is already built into the geocoding database installed with Tableau Desktop. These latitude and longitude fields will be displayed on the Data pane as measures and are how Tableau knows where to plot your data locations as you begin building a map (Figure 6.8). Note that in some advanced maps, you might elect to have your latitude and longitude coordinates be dimensions; these should be considered special uses and are not covered here.

Creating Geographic Hierarchies

In the Tableau worksheet space, if you have more than one level of geographic data in your dataset, you can create geographic hierarchies. While these are not critical to creating a map, geographic hierarchies allow you to quickly drill into the levels of detail your data contains. Because this dataset has both State and County, you can create a hierarchy using these two fields. State is the larger field in the hierarchy, so let's begin there.

To create a geographic hierarchy, right-click the field that represents the highest level of geographic data in the Data pane. Select Hierarchy > Create Hierarchy (Figure 6.9).

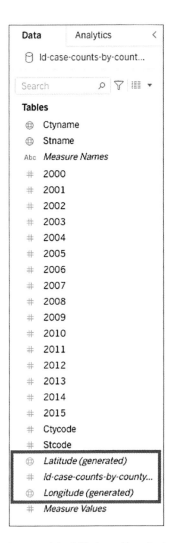

Figure 6.8 When Tableau recognizes geodata, latitude and longitude fields are automatically displayed as measures on the Data pane.

A dialog box appears that prompts you to name the hierarchy schema, such as Location. Enter a name and click OK.

A new field now appears in the Dimensions pane with the name of the hierarchy just created. The highest-level geographic data used to create the hierarchy—in this example, state—appears as the first rung in the hierarchy. To add additional fields, simply drag and drop into the hierarchy, placing them in correct order. Repeat as necessary until all geographic fields are included in the hierarchy. Figure 6.10 shows county has been added into the hierarchy below state.

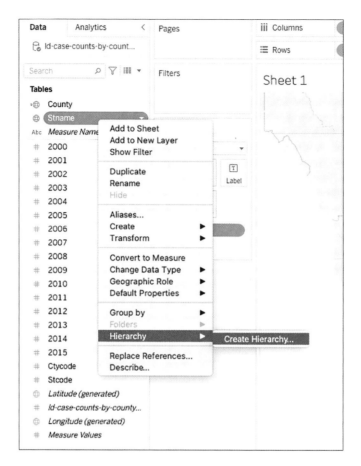

Figure 6.9 Creating hierarchies enables you to drill down to geographic levels of interest.

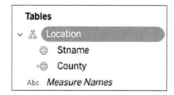

Figure 6.10 Example of a geographic hierarchy.

tip

Any date that follows a hierarchical structure (e.g., dates: year, quarter, month, day; product: category, product, sub-product) can be grouped into hierarchies to enable drill-down and drill-up functionality.

Proportional Symbol Maps

Proportional symbol maps are useful ways to show quantitative values for individual locations. They can show one or two quantitative values per location and can be encoded with visual cues like size and color. The proportional symbol map displaying the number of analytics academic programs across the United States shown in Chapter 1 is a great example of a symbol map (Figure 6.11).

> **note**
>
> You can download this public, and constantly updated, dataset from https://github.com/ryanswanstrom/awesome-datascience-colleges.

Figure 6.11 This symbol map shows the number and type of academic analytics programs available in the United States.

Let's create a new map together using the Lyme disease dataset. The first step is to give Tableau geographic coordinates to work with and lay the foundation of the map. Double-click the Latitude and Longitude generated fields under Measures. Latitude is added to the Rows shelf and Longitude to the Columns shelf. Initially, a blank map view is created (Figure 6.12).

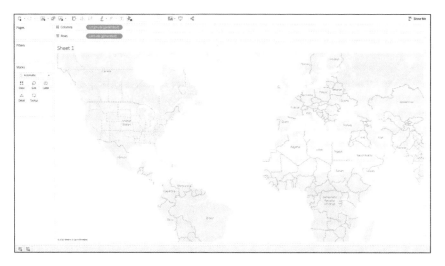

Figure 6.12 The first step in building a map visualization is to display the Latitude and Longitude coordinates to generate a blank map.

> tip
>
> Navigating maps on the Tableau canvas can be a little tricky. Use the controls shown in Figure 6.13 to help.

Figure 6.13 On-canvas map navigation controls.

Next, drag out the dimension that represents the location you want to plot your map by and drop it on the Details card. From the hierarchy group in this dataset, I've brought over County to look at Lyme disease cases at a more granular level. Thus, a lower level of detail is added to the view (Figure 6.14).

With a level of detail now on the map, the next step is to bring over the Measure to encode size. In this example, I am interested in seeing the number of Lyme disease cases per location, so I can simply bring the Total Number of Cases to the Size Marks card. With the size of the bubbles representing the number of Lyme disease cases in each county, we can visualize the range of values more clearly (Figure 6.15).

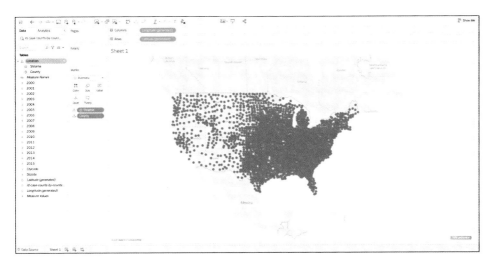

Figure 6.14 Add dimensions to the Detail Marks card to begin populating the data displayed on the map.

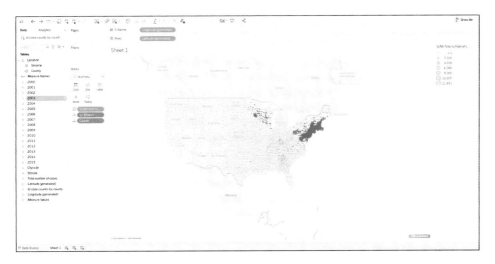

Figure 6.15 Adding detail to the Size Marks card can enhance the ways symbols appear on the map and encode additional data.

This is the basis of a proportional symbol map. The larger data points represent the locations with a larger total number of Lyme disease cases, and the smaller data points represent the locations with fewer cases.

Although this shows a good picture of program availability, a bit of additional formatting can help better visualize this data. The proportional symbol map is now complete (Figure 6.16).

Figure 6.16 Together, color and size can add significant layers of detail to a map.

At this point, your map should look similar to the one displayed in Figure 6.16. However, depending on which additional data you may have in your dataset, a few more tweaks can help to make the data in your map shine. Try the following:

- **For data with categories:** Sort your categories in an order that makes logical sense.

- **Color:** Adjust color and opacity, and add borders/halos as appropriate to clarify overlapping marks.

> tip
>
> Though we've accurately represented the data in terms of the total count of Lyme disease cases by county, we have failed to consider an important piece of context that's critical to mapping data. Context is everything. With maps, keeping population sizes in context is especially important. You might need to "normalize" your data with a calculated field to ensure you are looking at populations in the context of their geographic locations.
>
> Additionally, certain biases are inevitably embedded when mapping populations—representing *people*. See the "Keeping Maps Neutral" box later in this chapter for more on this issue.

Choropleth Map

A choropleth (or filled) map is a great tool for showing ratio or aggregated data. These maps use shading and coloring within geographic areas to encode values for quantities in those areas. A dataset for choropleth maps should include both quantitative and qualitative values, along with location information recognizable by Tableau.

Let's take our current symbol map and transform the data into a choropleth map. From here, we can simply use the Show Me card and select the choropleth map option to reimagine our data (Figure 6.17).

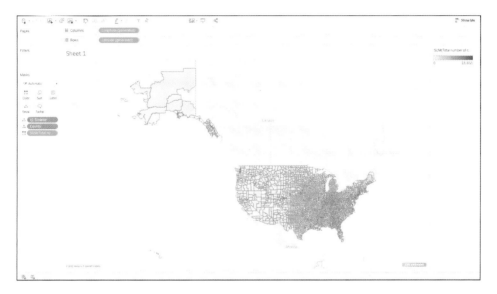

Figure 6.17 This is a nice example of why a choropleth can be a better alternative than a symbol map. There is simply too much data to show in individual points, but all of the data is necessary for accurate analysis.

Notice that the default aggregation type is SUM; however, this might not be the best fit depending on your data. Take a moment to verify that the field should be aggregated as a sum (because this is a count of disease cases reported, a sum is appropriate).

For clarity view, I've adjusted the map to show just the contiguous 48 states in Figure 6.18.

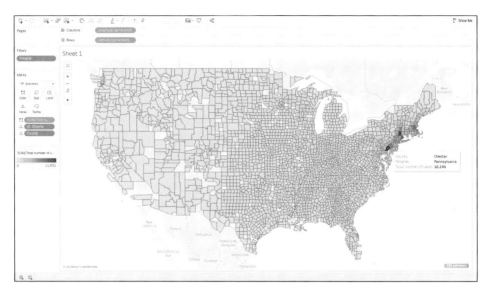

Figure 6.18 Color choice on a choropleth map is important and should follow the color practices described earlier in this text.

> **note**
>
> The level of detail specified in the map as well as the color distribution specified for the polygons affects how the data is represented and how people will interpret the data. In some cases, stepped color might be more appropriate.

MAP LAYERS

Of the many customization features for maps in Tableau, one of the most interesting is the choice of the built-in map background style to adjust the background of your map. The three background options offered in Tableau are Normal, Light (the default), and Dark. Figure 6.19 shows each background option. Tableau also offers street, outdoor, and satellite views for more detail, depending on the drill-down level represented in the map.

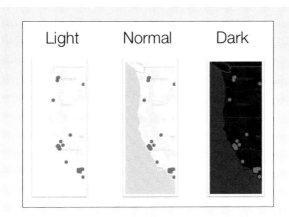

Figure 6.19 Three standard map backgrounds available in Tableau.

To select a Tableau map background style, choose Map > Background Maps or use the formatting pane to adjust the background style (Figure 6.20).

Figure 6.20 You can adjust map backgrounds and other formatting stylistics in the Background Layers pane.

You can also experiment with importing your own background map, adding a static background map image, and adding or subtracting map layers by data layers. Learn more at https://help.tableau.com/current/pro/desktop/en-us/maps_marks_layers.htm.

Additional map layers are available depending on the zoom level of the map (Figure 6.21).

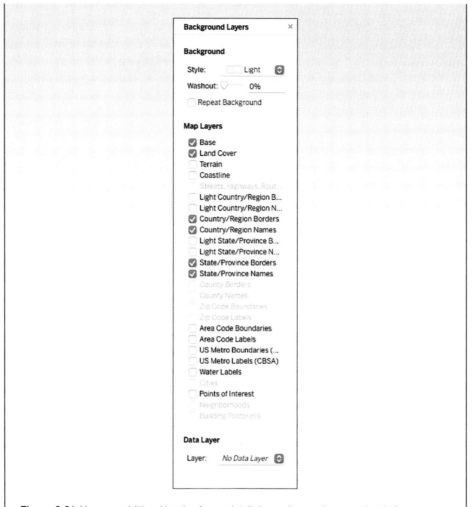

Figure 6.21 You can additional levels of map detail depending on the zoom level of your map.

KEEPING MAPS NEUTRAL

Visualizations are not neutral. Maps, like any storytelling device, can mislead audiences if they aren't designed correctly and honestly—and they can be customized for the audience. Google Maps does this with lines and by adjusting views for disputed territories. For example, Russian users see Crimea marked off with a solid line indicated that the area belongs to Russia, but for Ukrainian users the solid line is replaced with a dashed stroke indicating that the peninsula belongs to the Ukraine. Everyone else, including people in the United States, sees a hybrid line that reflects Crimea's disputed status (Figure 6.22).

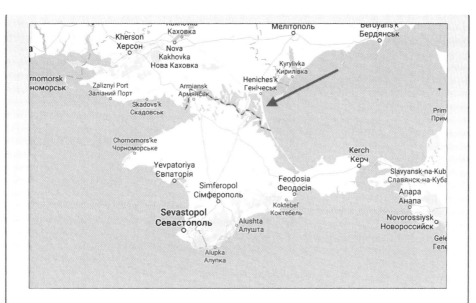

Figure 6.22 This Google Maps version of the Crimea border is intended for a U.S.-based audience and shows a hybrid line that reflects the border's disputed status.

Additionally, the manner in which we use shapes and colors to encode data that represents humans can be tricky on a map. One map of poverty in Minnesota recently changed from representing humans as red dots — which resulted in a map covered by an angry red swarm — to a gradient purple to look less aggressive (Figure 6.23).

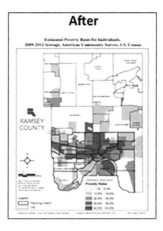

Figure 6.23 The initial, unfortunate design choice to represent population was later adjusted to a more neutral, and less offensive, approach.

These examples, and many more, speak to the importance of paying special attention to how our assumptions, intuitions, and biases—or even the things we might not consider—affect how we build visualizations to tell stories about people and places. Check out this article for more information: https://source. opennews.org/articles/when-designer-shows-design/.

Summary

This chapter explored ways to create fundamental maps displayed on the Show Me card in Tableau. The next chapter offers a pragmatic look at ways to curate meaningful visualizations that take advantage of the visual processing horsepower of the human brain.

CHAPTER 7

DESIGN TIPS FOR CURATING VISUAL ANALYTICS

Now that we've explored how to build fundamental data visualizations to communicate insights, this chapter dives into human cognition and visual perception to frame how pre-attentive attributes such as size, color, shape, and position affect the usability and efficacy of visual analytics. We will explore best practices for how design elements can be employed to direct an audience's attention and create a visual hierarchy of components to communicate effectively.

It's been said—by Tableau, actually—that data visualization is one of the most significant technologies of the 21st century. Of course, the act of visually representing data is not limited to the 21st century. Chapter 2 presented Minard's flow map of Napoleon's invasion of Russia, which was published in 1869 and is a prime example of the longevity of visual analytics. In addition to Minard's work, many other examples exist of people's attempts to visually explore, explain, and communicate data throughout the last several centuries. Many of these efforts have had significant influence on modern data visualization—from Ptolemy's earliest preserved use of a data table to display astronomical information in 150 BCE, to Descartes's 17th-century introduction of the Cartesian coordinate system, to Playfair's invention of the time-series line graph, bar chart, and pie chart in the 19th century, Nightingale's 1858 Coxcomb plot, Snow's map of the 1854 London cholera outbreak, and Tukey's box plot just a few decades ago (Figure 7.1). As far back as we can look, we seem to have sought visual ways to see and understand data more clearly.

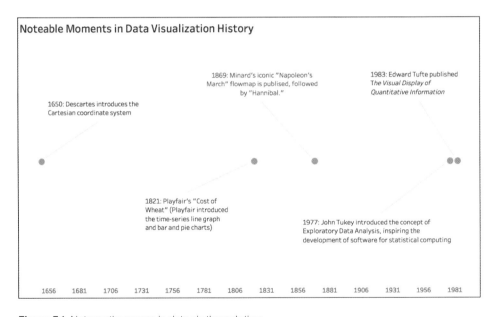

Figure 7.1 Noteworthy names in data viz through time.

Humans are intrinsically visual creatures. Of all the powerful processing systems hardwired into the human brain, none is more powerful than our visual system. Our brains are literally designed with cognitive and perceptual abilities to visually process complex information. We've been learning, remembering, and even writing (humans' earliest forms of written communications were visual languages such as cuneiform) using the power of pictures for nearly all of recorded human history. So, it makes sense that we would apply this same cognitive horsepower to how we interact with data.

note

John Medina, a developmental molecular biologist who studies how the mind reacts to and organizes information, developed the concept of the picture superiority effect, which recognizes that information learned by viewing pictures is more easily and more frequently recalled than that learned purely by textural or other word-form equivalents, including audio (Figure 7.2).

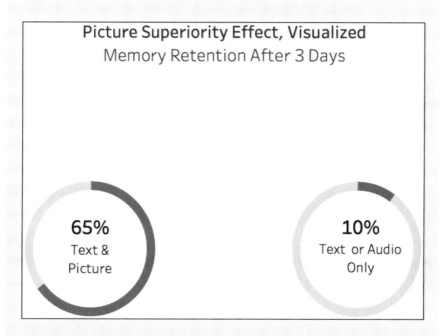

Figure 7.2 John Medina's picture superiority effect, visualized.

note

Read more on our shared visual human history, including a study of visual communication from cave drawings through advanced visualizations, in *The Visual Imperative: Creating a Visual Culture of Data Discovery* (Ryan, 2016).

The power of pictures isn't limited to helping us transform data into meaning. Visuals also act as memory magnets in our brains; we embed and retain memories in visual form. We're extremely good at this visual memorization: Research into our visual retention systems dating back as early as the 1970s has measured our visual memory capacity to be somewhere in the vicinity of 10,000 images, with a recognition rate of approximately 83%.

With that kind of retention power, one can easily understand how our visual capacity demands careful attention when working with data. We want to make sure that we are curating visual analytics as we apply design elements that leverage our cognitive abilities and help us better "see" our data insights.

Visual Design Building Blocks

We briefly covered pre-attentive features and perceptual pop-out in Chapter 2. Here, we'll take a deeper look at some of the fundamental ways that we can use these visual design building blocks to leverage our unique cognitive aspects that make visual analytics such powerful stimuli for the human brain. The steps you take to format your data visualizations and stories are critically important, as they can make or break the visual appeal and effectiveness of any visual communication.

As you might have noticed when we were building basic charts and maps presented on the Show Me card, you can format just about every visual element you see in Tableau. Choosing the right formatting is important to your analysis and your presentation, and Tableau allows analysts to customize the formatting for almost everything on a worksheet, including

- Titles, subtitles, and captions
- Annotations and tooltips
- Typeface fonts
- Colors
- Symbol shapes and sizes
- Lines (shading, alignment, borders, and graph lines)

All of these changes can be accomplished by using the Format pane and the Marks card in combination. Likewise, you can specify format settings for the entire worksheet, all rows, or all fields, or you can format individual parts of the view. Further, formatting choices can be applied at the worksheet or workbook level. This chapter takes a closer look at a few of the most important visual design building blocks and explores how you can use Tableau functionality to embed these visual cues purposefully and intuitively as you format your visualizations.

In particular, this chapter covers the following design elements:

- Color
- Lines
- Shapes

We'll examine additional formatting for dashboards and stories in a later chapter.

> **note**
>
> Before curating your visualization, you must first understand and explore the data, and represent it using the chart or graph best suited for your data's story. From there, you can apply visual cues that enable you to intuitively and meaningfully communicate the desired insights to your audience. Chapter 5, "Fundamental Data Visualizations," and Chapter 9, "Beyond Fundamentals: Advanced Visualizations," cover selecting and building the best charts.

'PROPER()' STRING FUNCTION

A common data preparation task in datasets—particularly those with many dimensions (e.g., names, categories)—is often formatting the case of the text. Text data may be exported as, or otherwise converted to, all capital letters or all lowercase letters. While there are a variety of ways to address proper case format for text fields, Tableau 2022.4 includes a simple, yet powerful, new function to convert strings to the proper case.

The function 'PROPER()' is a simple calculated field that transforms string data. It capitalizes the first letter of a text string and any letters following non-letter characters and converts the rest to lowercase (Figure 7.3).

Figure 7.3 This simple calculated field transforms string data into proper sentence case.

Color

Color is one of the most important, most complicated, and most frequently misused elements of data visualization. When used well, color can enhance and clarify a visualization; when used poorly, it can confuse, misrepresent, or obstruct clear communication. Color is such a critical element in representing data visually that Tableau employs color scientists to help design the best color palettes and to provide deep education on the appropriate use of color. This section covers best practices for properly applying color to a visual that aligns to its data and your story. While we can only scratch the surface of color application within the scope of this book, this is an area in which you should invest more time learning.

All marks in Tableau have a default color, even if no fields are placed on the Color Marks card. For most marks, blue is the default color. For text, gray is the default color.

We'll explore how to use the Color Marks card when looking at how it is used in different types of visualization.

> **note**
>
> The visuals in this section use the Global Superstore dataset, which is available from the Connect to Data screen in Tableau.

Tableau applies color depending on the field's values. For discrete values, or dimensions, Tableau typically uses a categorical palette; for continuous values, or measures, it assigns a quantitative palette. These translate into the three primary ways to encode data with color in data visualization:

- Sequential
- Diverging for continuous, quantitative values
- Categorical for discrete values

Sequential Color

Sequential color encodes a quantitative value from low to high using gradients of a single color and is applied when either all values are positive or all values are negative. A great example of this is sales data, which go from zero to infinity. The map in Figure 7.4 uses a sequential color scale to encode positive sales amounts into each U.S. state.

Figure 7.4 This map uses sequential color to show the sum of sales from least to greatest. The darker the blue, the higher the sales are.

The automatic sequential color palette used in Tableau is blue. In addition to changing the palette itself, you can adjust the distribution of color by clicking the Color Marks card, which opens the Edit Colors dialog box (Figure 7.5).

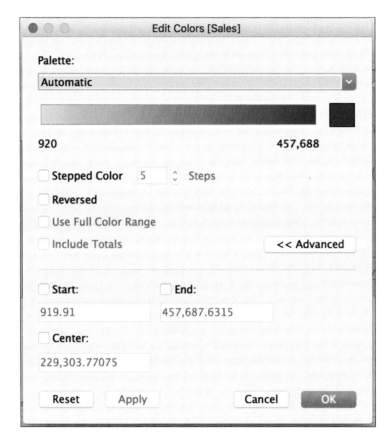

Figure 7.5 Select and adjust color palettes in the Edit Colors dialog box.

Diverging Color

Diverging color encodes a quantitative value but has a midpoint (for example, zero). Numbers on either side of this midpoint (positive and negative) are displayed in a different color, with each having its own sequential palette.

Figure 7.6 uses a diverging color palette to display profit by state (top) and profit by product category and subcategory (bottom). Positive profit is colored blue, with darker blue reflecting higher profit. Profit could also be negative, and in this visual, negative values are encoded in orange, with the darker orange reflecting a bigger loss.

Figure 7.6 Diverging color palettes display positive and negative values using gradient shading of two contrasting colors to encode values.

Similarly to the sequential color palette, Tableau automatically assigns a color palette for diverging values. The default is an orange–blue diverging color palette (we discuss why you should *not* use a red–green diverging color palette and instead use better palettes to avoid issues with color vision deficiency later in this chapter). As with any palette, you can adjust the diverging colors (Figure 7.7).

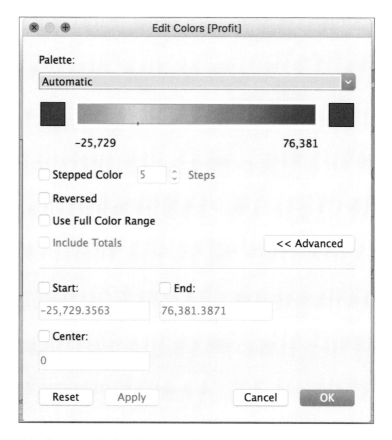

Figure 7.7 Using the automatic diverging orange–blue color palette is best practice.

Diverging color palettes are clearly designated in the Tableau color library. Beyond changing the colors themselves, you can adjust the midpoint. Midpoints do not have to be zero. They could be the average, such that color values are then above or below average, or a target, such that color values then exceed or fall below that point.

Stepped Color

In addition to changing the range of colors, you can group values into color-coded bins using stepped colors. Use the up and down arrows to specify how many bins to create (Figure 7.8).

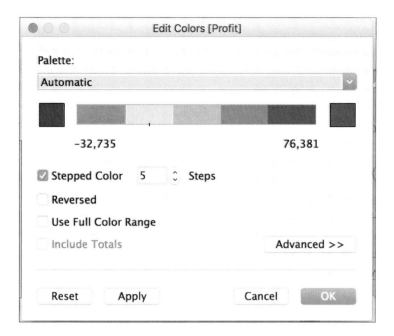

Figure 7.8 Rather than use gradient shading, you can use stepped color palettes to distinguish colors.

Reversed Color

If it makes sense to do so, you can select the Reversed option to reverse the order of colors in the range. For sequential colors, this means darkening the intensity for the lower values rather than for the higher values. Likewise, for diverging colors, this means swapping the two colors in the palette in addition to reversing the shades within each range.

Categorical Color

Categorical colors encode categories (e.g., apples, bananas, and oranges; shoes, socks, and shirts) using distinct colors appropriate for fields that have no inherent quantitative order (Figure 7.9).

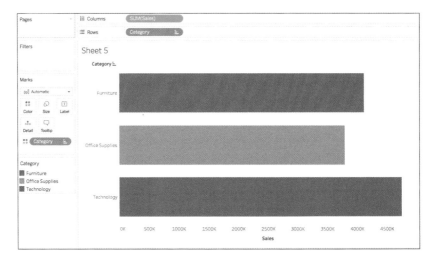

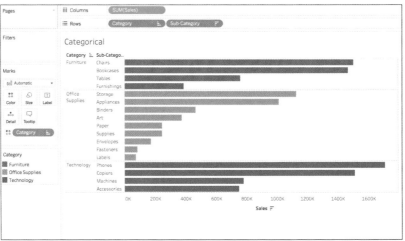

Figure 7.9 These examples use the Tableau automatic palette for categorical color coding.

By default, Tableau assigns categorical color using the automatic Tableau color palette. As you might expect, you can adjust this to use a color palette of your own choosing. To change color values, click the Color Marks card and select Edit. A dialog box opens that allows you to select from the color palettes in Tableau (Figure 7.10). You can assign an entirely new palette to every item in the field, or you can manually assign a color to each field by selecting and assigning a color swatch to individual items. If you need to manually add a specific color shade to comply with company branding guidelines, you can do that by applying a custom color palette.

Figure 7.10 The Tableau color library includes a wide variety of preprogrammed color palettes to choose from. You can also program your own.

Color Effects

Beyond advanced color options, additional configuration options not related to the actual colors shown are available in Tableau. These include adjusting opacity, mark borders, and mark halos (Figure 7.11). The preceding chapter explored some of these functions briefly within the context of curating maps.

Figure 7.11 The Color Marks card offers additional options for color formatting.

Opacity

Adjusting opacity can be helpful for looking at dense scatter plots or in maps overlaying a background image. Moving the slider left makes the marks become more transparent. Consider the before and after maps in Figure 7.12: The map on the top has opacity at 100%, whereas the opacity in the map on the bottom is at 50%. You can also use this technique to ensure that overlapping marks do not become lost amidst competing data.

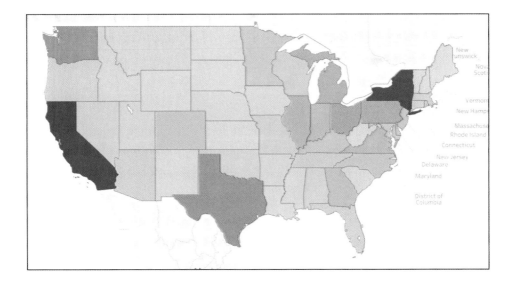

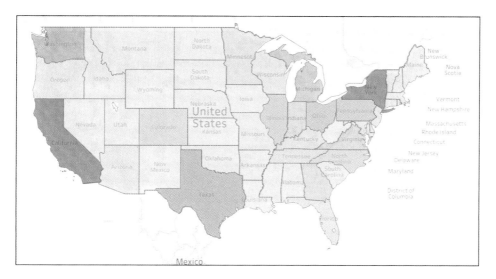

Figure 7.12 Adjusting the opacity of color can be a helpful way to show layers without obscuring marks in the visualization. This is especially helpful in maps and scatter plots, which might have many layers of data or overlapping marks in one viz.

Mark Borders

Tableau automatically displays all marks without borders; however, you can turn borders on for all mark types except text, line, and shapes.

Borders can be helpful in distinguishing closely spaced marks—but they can also make it more difficult to distinguish color-encoded dimensions because they make marks narrower (as in a stacked bar chart). Adjust your visualization with and without borders to see whether they add or reduce clarity.

Mark Halos

Mark halos can assist in making marks more visible, particularly on maps. They surround each mark with a ring of contrasting color (Figure 7.13).

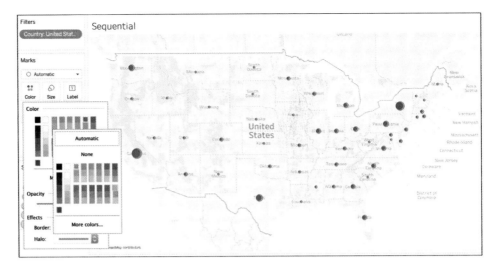

Figure 7.13 Mark halos create a "ring" around a data point and increase its visibility and separation from other marks on the viz.

Pre-attentive Colors

Color should be used not just strategically, but sparingly. Research says that the human brain can differentiate approximately eight colors at a time, but best practices suggest that using simple color palettes of five or fewer colors reduces the stress on a user to decipher the meaning of color in a visualization. Many data visualizations never require more than two to three colors, including gray.

One way to employ strategic, sparing use of color is to use color to highlight data or alert audiences to important insights. You use a *highlight* color to highlight one data point or category. For example, suppose you are tracking profits of product categories over time, with a separate line representing each category, and you want to highlight the consistent high profits in a certain category—perhaps technology. You can highlight one state by coloring only this line and using gray for the other categories (Figure 7.14). This allows the audience to clearly see how well this category is doing in comparison to others on the chart. Earth-tone colors, such as blue, are great colors for highlighting.

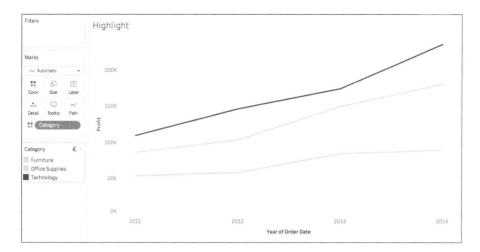

Figure 7.14 Using a highlighting color, such as blue, drives attention to one mark on a viz without the need for additional labeling.

Similarly to highlighting, you can use *alerting* colors to draw the audience's attention to a particular data point. Using the same line chart as in Figure 7.14, rather than highlighting the high profits of the technology category, suppose the goal is to alert the audience to the low profits in the furniture category (Figure 7.15). In this use case, alerting is done with an alarming or alerting color, such as red or orange, to indicate to the audience that something is wrong.

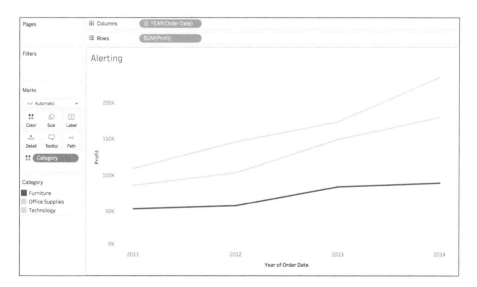

Figure 7.15 Using an alerting color, such as red, drives attention to one mark on a viz without the need for additional labeling.

It's important to note that in Western culture, red is often associated with negative values or associations. However, this is not always consistent with color culture in other countries, such as China. Bright alerting colors could be red, orange, or yellow.

Cultural color connotations are but one special consideration we need to keep in mind when using color in visual analytics. Let's take a look at a few more.

Important Color Considerations

Colors hold meaning, even when they are not attached to data. A certain amount of psychology is involved in understanding color, as well as cultural connotations, tone, and differences in how people see and interpret color.

- **Color psychology:** The *Color Harmony Compendium* by Terry Marks and Tina Sutton provides a comprehensive look at color psychology—how human emotion, memory, and embedded cultural connotations affect how we "understand" and react to color. Blue, for example, is the most liked of all colors, typically perceived as positive, while orange is high energy and can convey warning symbols—just one explanation for why blue–orange is the best-practice palette for diverging information. Red, in addition to being the most vibrant color in the spectrum, tends to make people hungry (consider the use of red in food packaging and fast-food logos). Gray is often seen as a mature authoritative color, and a strong secondary color choice.

- **Cultural color connotations:** When selecting colors for international audiences, it's important to consider the connotations that colors may carry in other parts of the world. For example, while most Western culture associate warnings, danger, and other negative values with red, many Eastern colors see red as instead connoting wealth and good fortune. A great resource for unstinting cultural color connotations is David McCandless's cultural color chart, which can be found in his book *The Visual Miscellaneum: A Colorful Guide to the World's Most Consequential Trivia*.

- **Employing "brand" colors:** Many visual analysts working within a corporate structure may find themselves tasked with using company brand palettes. Sometimes these brand palettes may stand in direct contrast to established color-use best practices or encourage use that would otherwise disagree with the color applications discussed in this book. One recommendation for navigating problematic brand colors is to identify one or two appropriate colors from the palette to utilize as highlight or alert colors, and to rely on black, gray, and white space for the rest.

- **Color consistency:** One important principle in visual analytics is consistency— that is, the notion that once you adopt a principle or method, you should continue to follow it consistently. This is especially important when it comes to color. Once you've established the meaning of a color cue, continue to use it consistently throughout all visualizations in a series, a dashboard, or a story. A change in color signifies a change in meaning and could confuse your audience unnecessarily.

The Truth About Red and Green

Designing with the potential for color vision deficiencies in mind is such a large consideration that it demands its own section. Most of us are familiar with the "traffic light" palette, where red is stop (or bad), green is go (or positive), and yellow or orange (or white as a midpoint) means to proceed with caution.

Although this option is available in Tableau, there is very rarely, *if ever*, a valid and compelling reason to use it. Instead, a very compelling reason exists *not* to use it: color vision deficiency (CVD). For the most part, we all share a common color vision sensory experience. However, as many as 8% of men and 0.5% of women suffer from some kind of CVD. Most prolific among these deficiencies is red–green, or deuteranope, making this palette particularly troublesome. Even if the red–green palette *must* be used, techniques can be applied to make this color palette appropriate for circumventing CVD issues, such as using a blue–green rather than a pure green, which will help make the colors distinct enough that they can be recognized by someone with CVD.

Take a look at Figure 7.16. The highlight table on the left will appear red–green to someone without CVD—but to someone with deuteranope, the colors appear as the image on the right. As you can tell, the colors in the table on the left are much less distinct to someone with red–green CVD , which reduces the potency of the visualization. The same is true of using red–blue divergent color palettes, which still fall below the blue–orange best practice option.

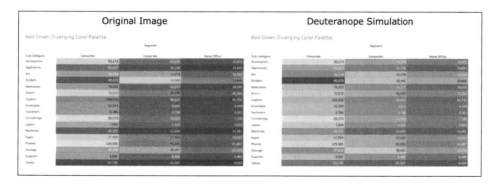

Figure 7.16 A red–green image is virtually unreadable to someone with deuteranope color deficiency.

To provide an easy solution for navigating the complexity of CVDs, Tableau has both an orange–blue diverging color palette (for quantitative values) and a color-blind palette (for categorical values). Figure 7.17 illustrates these color palettes.

tip

To experiment with how your own visuals might appear to someone with various types of color vision deficiencies, visit www.vischeck.com.

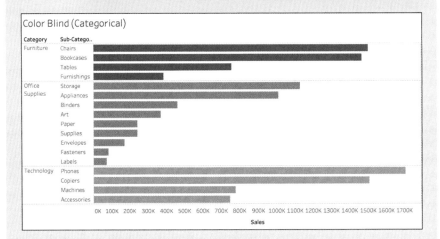

Figure 7.17 An orange–blue color palette is best suited to mitigating any color deficiency issues.

USING TITLES AS COLOR LEGENDS

Chart titles and subtitles provide an interesting opportunity to embed a color legend. Consider the example displayed in Figure 7.18. In this bar chart, the color legend on the right could be eliminated completely to give more real estate to the visual without losing any important information.

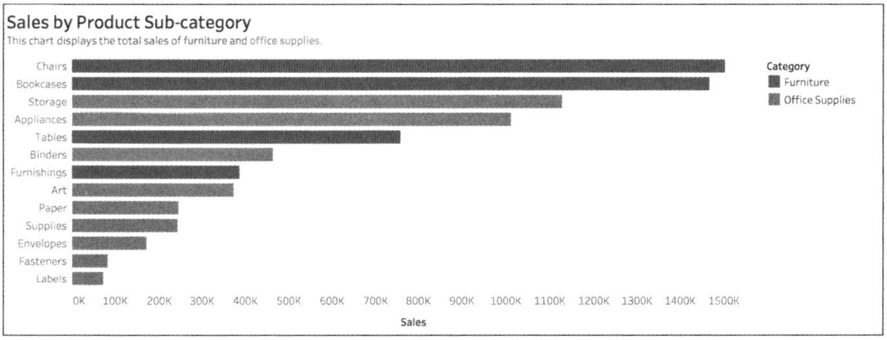

Figure 7.18 Rather than using a traditional legend, chart titles and descriptions provide an interesting opportunity to embed color legends.

Lines

Lines have several purposes in data visualizations. They act as guides, they reinforce patterns, they provide direction, and they create shapes. As with any visual element, too many lines—or lines given too much emphasis—can cause distraction or confusion. However, used wisely, they can be transformative. Like color, lines should be used sparingly to reduce the amount of ink onscreen so that the data can lead the story.

This section covers ways to format lines within individual visualizations in Tableau and make effective use of them as view lines (axis lines, reference lines, and so on), borders, and shaded bands. It also looks at how lines can affect visualizations in the form of gridlines, axis rulers, and panes.

To format lines in Tableau worksheets, select the Format menu, then the part of the view that you want to format (Figure 7.19).

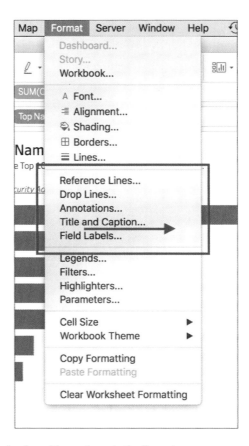

Figure 7.19 Access the line formatting options via the Format menu.

You can also right-click on your sheet and select Format (Figure 7.20).

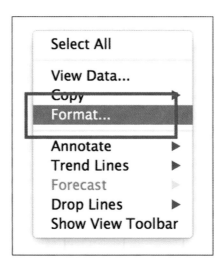

Figure 7.20 You can also right-click the worksheet and select the Format option to access the line formatting options.

Either of these methods opens the Format pane as a new tab in place of the Data pane, with icons to help direct formatting of individual elements in the worksheet (Figure 7.21).

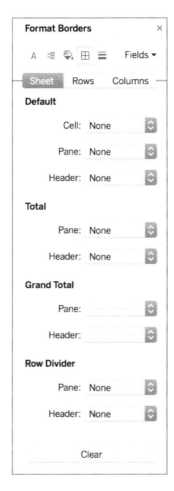

Figure 7.21 Once activated, the Format Borders pane opens in place of the Data pane.

note

The visualizations in this section were created using a Tableau-provided dataset of the most popular male and female baby names in each state from 1910 to 2012. This data is collected by the Social Security Administration.

By default, most chart types in Tableau include gray axis lines, zero lines, drop lines, and borders. If added, reference lines that help you analyze statistical information in the data are also gray by default.

In general, a best practice is to remove as many of these lines as possible, keeping only those truly necessary to guide audiences through the visualization or highlight important aspects of the data.

Let's walk through the steps of formatting lines using a series of simple visualizations.

Formatting Grid Lines, Zero Lines, and Drop Lines

Grid lines, zero lines, and drop lines connect marks to the axis. You format them using the lines icon on the Format pane, and you can adjust them by sheet, row, or column (Figure 7.22).

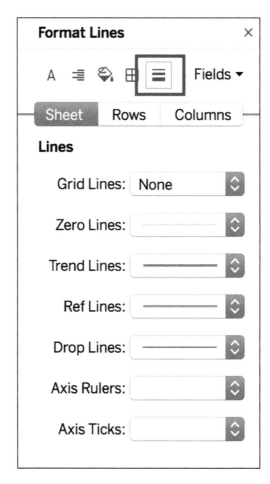

Figure 7.22 Format grid lines, zero lines, and other reference lines using the Lines icon on the Format pane.

Figure 7.23 is the default view of a sorted bar chart of the top 10 girls' baby names in the United States from 1910 to 2012. (Titles/subtitles are formatted by double-clicking on the default title line.) We will use this visualization to experiment with formatting lines.

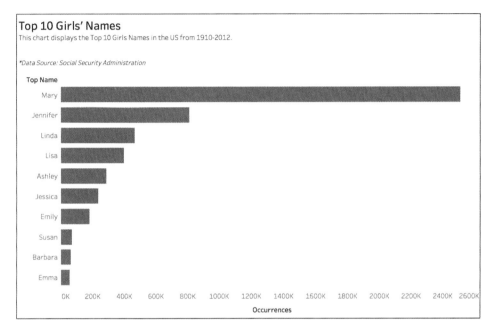

Top 10 Girls' Names
This chart displays the Top 10 Girls Names in the US from 1910-2012.

Data Source: Social Security Administration

Figure 7.23 A simple bar chart of top baby names, without line formatting.

To create this chart, follow these steps:

1. Filter the data by Gender, selecting Female.
2. Drag Occurrences (SUM) to Columns and Top Name to Rows.
3. Sort Top Name in descending order by Occurrence.
4. Filter by Top Name, using the Top filter by Field to select top 10 by Gender.
5. You might also adjust the view to Entire View.

Selecting which lines to remove is a matter of judgment. Typically, I remove all grid lines. You can eliminate zero lines, too, but whether you choose to remove this line should depend on how important being above or below zero is in your data.

In this example, I removed all grid lines, zero lines, reference, and drop lines. I also removed axis ticks and row axis rulers, but kept the column axis rulers for reference and reformatted them as dotted lines (Figure 7.24).

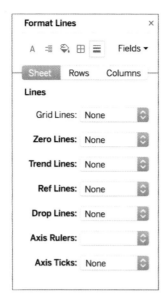

Figure 7.24 You can format lines at the sheet, row, and column levels.

The resulting visualization is much cleaner, with only one line at the bottom of the x-axis, as shown in Figure 7.25.

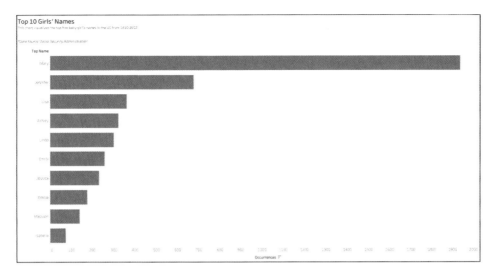

Figure 7.25 A simple bar chart of top baby names, with line formatting.

We could take this visual a step further, based on our previous discussion of color, and eliminate unnecessary use of color to highlight the most common girl's name of the time period under review (Figure 7.26). In this slightly modified (and updated) visualization, I've also adjusted the column zero line to be a thin gray line so as to better separate the variables.

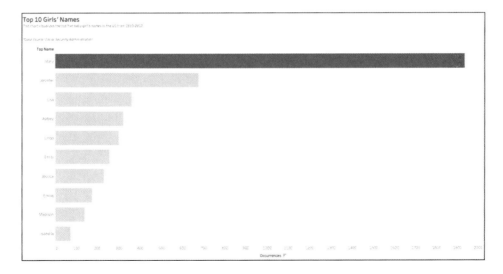

Figure 7.26 Takes formatting a bit further to provide a clearer message with the visualization.

Formatting Borders

Borders are the lines that surround visualizations, demarking the table, pane, cells, and headers. You can specify the border style, width, and color to format the cell, pane, and header areas using the grid icon on the Format pane (Figure 7.27).

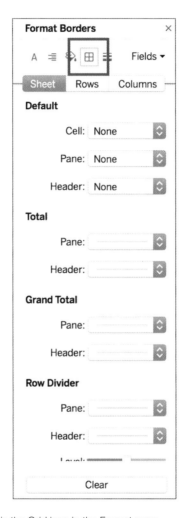

Figure 7.27 Format borders via the Grid icon in the Format pane.

Returning to the bar chart, I have added orange row dividers as borders to show how they appear when formatted (Figure 7.28). Notice that because I changed the format of the axis line to a dotted line, it now appears as colored dots.

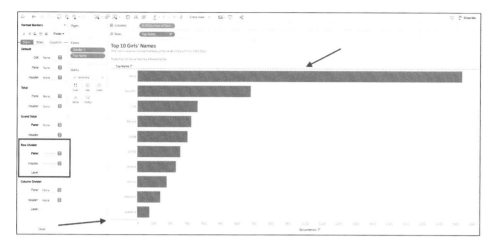

Figure 7.28 This figure shows an example of border formatting for row dividers.

Row and column dividers are most commonly used in nested data tables, because they serve to visually break up a view and separate data fields, especially when several levels of data exist. Figure 7.29 is the default view of a nested data table reflecting the top 10 girls' and boys' baby names from 1910 to 2012. (Titles/subtitles are formatted by double-clicking on the default title line.)

Top Baby Names 1910-2012
Data Source: Social Security Administration

Gender	Top Name	
Female	Mary	2,510,913
	Jennifer	811,054
	Linda	465,969
	Lisa	396,100
	Ashley	287,670
	Jessica	233,289
	Emily	181,136
	Susan	69,966
	Barbara	62,384
	Emma	55,096
Male	Michael	2,274,105
	James	1,566,897
	Robert	1,213,750
	John	756,249
	David	291,260
	Jacob	201,448
	Christopher	192,699
	William	111,884
	Daniel	69,552
	Jason	63,069

Figure 7.29 A basic nested data table, without additional formatting.

To create this table, follow these steps:

1. Drag Gender and Top Name to Rows.
2. Drag Occurrences (SUM) to the Text Marks card.
3. Sort Top Name in descending order by Occurrence.
4. Use the method described earlier to filter the top variables, or scroll through the table and select all names after the first 10 for each gender, right-click, and select Hide.

Using the Format Borders function, you can modify the style, width, color, and level of the borders that divide each row or each column by using the row and column divider drop-down menus. The level refers to the header level you want to divide by. At the highest level, all fields are divided (as shown in Figure 7.29, which is divided by Top Name at the highest level).

Having as many lines as appear in Figure 7.29 is unnecessary, even in a table. Thus, at the sheet level, I've reformatted the row dividers to a Level 2 heading so that I can differentiate between genders rather than separating each name. At the column level, I've also removed the column divider on the right to simplify the table's appearance (Figure 7.30).

Figure 7.30 Formatting lines at several levels requires individual attention to each level.

The resulting table, shown in Figure 7.31, is both cleaner and easier to read.

Top Baby Names 1910-2012
Data Source: Social Security Administration

Gender	Top Name	
Female	Mary	2,510,913
	Jennifer	811,054
	Linda	465,969
	Lisa	396,100
	Ashley	287,670
	Jessica	233,289
	Emily	181,136
	Susan	69,966
	Barbara	62,384
	Emma	55,096
Male	Michael	2,274,105
	James	1,566,897
	Robert	1,213,750
	John	756,249
	David	291,260
	Jacob	201,448
	Christopher	192,699
	William	111,884
	Daniel	69,552
	Jason	63,069

Figure 7.31 A simple data table, with some considerate line formatting.

Formatting, Shading, and Banding

At the intersection of lines and color, you can use shading to set a background color for the entire visualization or for various areas of importance, such as headers, panes, or totals.

Shaded areas are a technique commonly used to create banding, where the background color alternates from row to row or from column to column. This technique is useful for tables (as shown in Figure 7.31) because it helps the eye distinguish rows or columns more intuitively than added superfluous lines. To format shading and banding, you use the paint can icon on the Format pane (Figure 7.32).

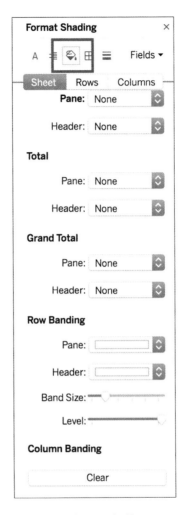

Figure 7.32 Format shading via the paint can icon on the Format pane.

The nested table in Figure 7.31 has row banding by default. If desired, you could change this choice by sliding the band size to zero (Figure 7.33).

You can explore additional banding options by interacting with the various settings on the Format pane. As a guide, practice with the following:

- **Pane and header:** This affects the color of the bands.
- **Band size:** This affects the thickness of the bands.
- **Level:** If you have nested tables or multiple dimensions, this option allows you to add and format banding at specific levels.

Figure 7.33 You can adjust row banding manually on the Format pane.

REMOVING FIELD LABELS AND UNNECESSARY HEADERS

By default, when you create a visualization, Tableau provides both field labels and headers for each axis. Often, this is redundant, especially when you add a title to your chart. Removing unnecessary elements streamlines the visualization for your audience.

As an example, reconsider Figure 7.25. You can see the field labels for Top Name rows, as well as the axis header for Occurrences directly below the count. Does your audience need this duplicated information, or can we trust them to infer the fields without an additional header? If the latter is true, consider right-clicking on the field label for Top Name and removing it. Next, to remove the axis header, right-click to Edit Axis and remove the title by erasing the text in the field. The resulting visualization is much simpler (Figure 7.34).

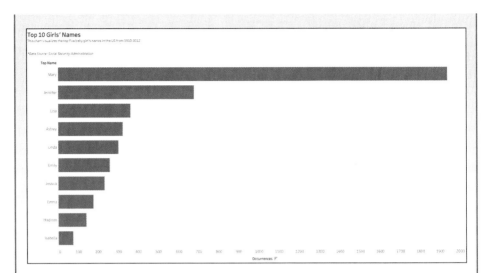

Figure 7.34 A modified view of a simple bar chart after eliminating redundant headers.

For additional simplification, you can remove the *x*-axis entirely, and label the individual bars instead (Figure 7.35).

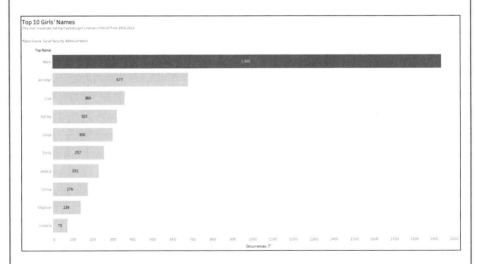

Figure 7.35 With some final polish and curation, this bar chart is data-rich and ink-minimal.

Figure 7.36 shows before and after views of the original and finished versions of this chart.

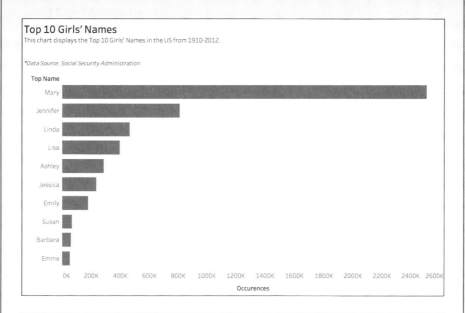

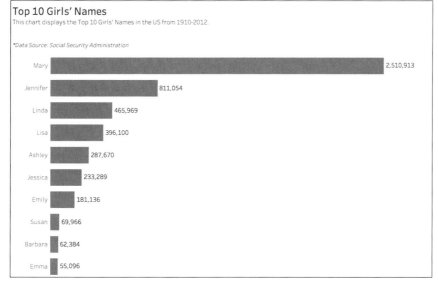

Figure 7.36 Before and after views of the Top 10 Girls' Names bar chart.

> **tip**
>
> Reinstating a previously removed header can be a bit of a trick in Tableau. To unhide a header, select Analysis > Table Layout. You can also unhide any header from the rows or columns by simply right-clicking on the pill. Use the header's check box to toggle the header's display on or off for each pill.

Shapes

As a time-saving technique, shapes are one of the ways that our brains recognize patterns. We immediately group similar objects and separate them from those that look different. Some chart types, such as packed bubble charts, use shapes (along with size and color) to encode meaning. Additionally, we can use shapes in interesting ways to personalize data stories in Tableau. The two ways to use shapes in Tableau are with the Shape Marks card and with custom shapes.

Shape Marks Card

The Shape Marks card feature allows you to assign different shapes to data marks. Dropping a dimension on the Shape Marks card prompts Tableau to assign a unique shape to each member in the field, as well as display a shape legend (Figure 7.37). Using the Size Marks card allows you to enlarge or reduce the size of each shape mark.

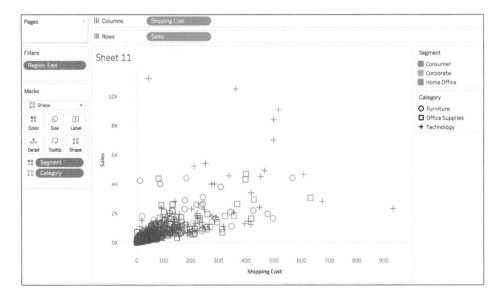

Figure 7.37 The Size Marks card allows you to use shapes to encode categories, a helpful technique on a crowded scatter plot.

As shown in Figure 7.37, the default shapes in Tableau are unfilled symbols. This palette contains 10 unique shapes. If your data includes more than 10 values, the shapes will repeat.

You can edit this default palette and assign a different palette from the library of shape options within Tableau. Choices include a variety of shape palettes, arrows, weather symbols, and KPI metrics. To edit the shape palette assigned to your data, click the Shape Marks card and select Edit Shape. A dialog box, similar to the Color dialog box, appears that allows you to select a new palette as well as manually assign shapes to each data item (Figure 7.38).

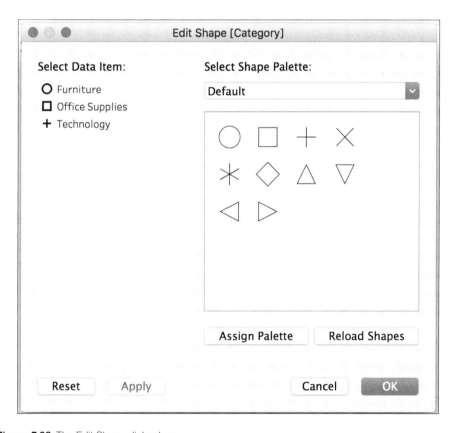

Figure 7.38 The Edit Shape dialog box.

Custom Shapes

If none of the palettes in the Tableau library appeals to you or is suitable for your dataset, you can add custom shapes into your Tableau environment for use in your workbooks. Custom shapes can add a nice design touch to your visualization, particularly when you are building a narrative or working to create engagement or visual appeal.

This function requires accessing the Tableau Repository on your machine. To add custom shape palettes into the Tableau library, follow these steps:

1. Create your image files. Each shape should be its own file, and most image formats (including .png, .gif, .jpg, .bmp, and .tiff) are acceptable. (Tableau does not support symbols in .emf format.)

2. Copy the shape files to a new folder in the My Tableau Repository > Shapes folder on your computer. The name of the folder will be the name of the new palette in Tableau.

> note
>
> If you plan to use color to encode shapes, use a transparent background in your image file (.png). Otherwise, the entire square of the symbol thumbnail will be colored, rather than just the symbol itself.

Figure 7.39 shows that I have added two new palettes, Harry Potter and Hogwarts House Crests, to my shape library.

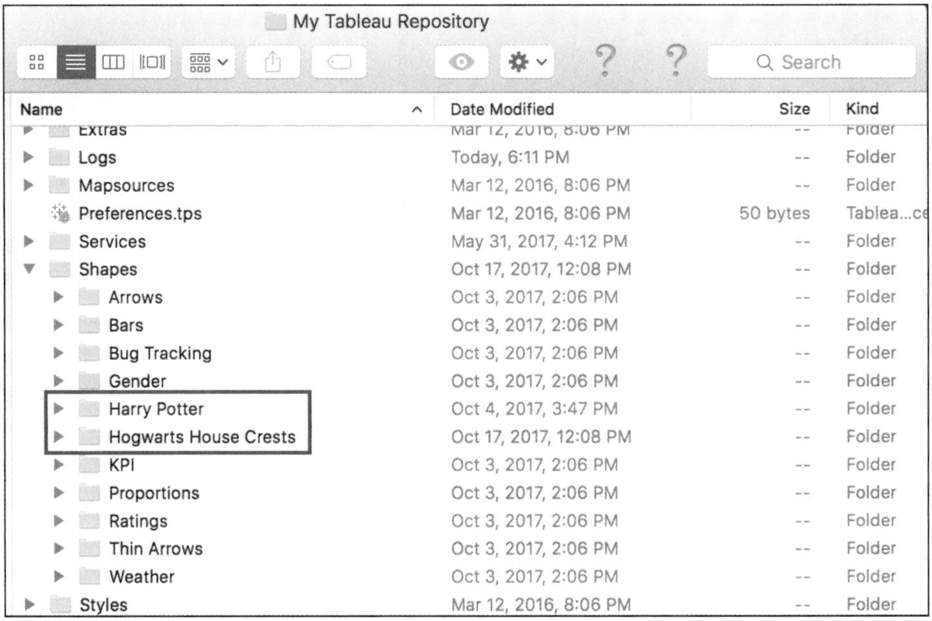

Figure 7.39 You can manually add shape palettes to Tableau's shape library by dropping them into the Shapes folder in your Tableau Repository.

When you return to Tableau, you will see the new palettes included in the Shape Palette library in the Edit Shape dialog box. If you modified the shapes while Tableau was running, you might need to click Reload Shapes (Figure 7.40).

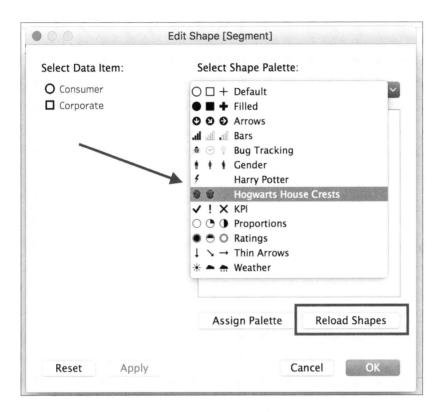

Figure 7.40 Manually added shapes now appear in the Edit Shape dialog box.

You can assign these new shapes in the same manner as you do any shape palette within Tableau.

> tip
>
> For tips on creating custom shapes best suited for use in Tableau, see the helpful article at www.tableau.com/drive/custom-shapes.

Image Roles
Tableau 2022.4 introduced the ability to add web images dynamically to worksheets by including image URLs within datasets. These images can be used in headers to add visual detail to the analysis.

Image roles can be assigned to discrete dimension fields. A few steps are necessary to ensure these assets display properly in Tableau. First and foremost, make sure your image fields meet the Tableau requirements to be assigned an image role:

- URLs must navigate to image files with .png, .jpeg, or .jpg file extensions.
- Each URL should begin with http or https as the transfer protocol. (If this information isn't included, Tableau will assume https.)
- As many as 500 images can be loaded per field.
- Each image file should be smaller than 128 kilobytes.

Assigning an image role to a field containing image URLs is achieved in the same way as assigning any data role (see Chapter 8). That is, in either the Data source page or a worksheet, click the data icon and select Image Role > URL (Figure 7.41).

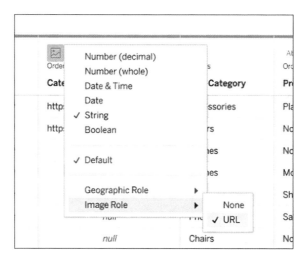

Figure 7.41 Assigning an image role to a field containing image URLs is done by clicking the data icon and selecting Image Role > URL.

With this data role selected, you can drop the corresponding pill onto your worksheet canvas to see the images along with their associated data in your visualization (Figure 7.42).

note

All data lacking a URL has been excluded for illustration purposes.

Figure 7.42 A visualization that now includes images associated with data using image roles.

Summary

This chapter discussed ways to format important visual cues in data visualization that can enhance your data's story. The next chapter covers preparing data for visual analysis in Tableau before we begin exploring additional formatting options in Tableau to take our visual analytics to the next level as data stories.

CHAPTER 8

STRUCTURING ANALYTICS FOR STORYTELLING: PREP, DASHBOARDS, AND STORIES

Knowing the basics of visual analysis—from understanding your data's context to knowing when to use fundamental charts and graphs to following design tips for effective curation—better prepares you to begin visually exploring your data to craft compelling data visualizations and narratives that deliver your analysis to its intended audience. However, before you can start working with real data in Tableau, you need to be sure it is in the right shape for analysis. Most, if not all, data needs a little bit of work before you're ready to get hands-on in Tableau.

This chapter moves beyond the basics of visual analytics to take our first steps in architecting outputs of analysis in visual data dashboards and stories. We'll begin by taking a closer look at how to prepare data in Tableau and what to do about messy survey data—a common experience for data storytellers. Then we'll start building data dashboards and stories that incorporate features such as filters, annotations, and highlights to present compelling, meaningful, and actionable outcomes of visual analytics.

Basic Data Prep in Tableau: Data Interpreter

Like its predecessor versions, Tableau 2022 includes built-in data preparation capabilities that help make reshaping data a smoother and less labor-intensive experience than doing it by hand (or using the no-longer-supported Tableau Excel add-in, which worked only for Windows-based licenses). While a full course in data preparation is beyond the scope of this book, before getting into a specific data prep exercise using survey data, we'll review some of the basic data preparation tools included in Tableau. We took a superficial look at Data Interpreter in Chapter 3, "Getting Started with Tableau," but this section takes a more in-depth look at how it can be used with a real dataset.

Data Interpreter is a built-in prep resource in Tableau Desktop that helps to automatically eliminate common formatting issues when importing data from Excel, CSV, PDF, and Google Sheets. While the data may be nicely prepared in those tools, spreadsheets like these often include aesthetic touches intended to make data easier to read, such as titles, stacked headers, extra columns, and so forth. Unfortunately, these attributes, when imported into an analytics tools, introduce common formatting errors that can affect analysis and that need to be eliminated before moving forward.

This exercise uses a dataset titled "Significant Volcanic Eruptions." This sampled dataset comprises open data and contains a global listing of more than 600 volcanic eruptions from 4360 BC to the present stored in the Significant Volcanic Eruptions Database. Within this data, a significant eruption is classified as one that meets at least one of the following criteria: caused fatalities, caused moderate damage (approximately $1 million or more), Volcanic Explosivity Index (VEI) of 6 or greater, generated a tsunami, or was associated with a significant earthquake.

> ### note
>
> The Significant Volcanic Eruptions dataset is a relatively clean dataset that can be found in Tableau's library of sample datasets at https://public.tableau.com/app/resources/sample-data. For instructional purposes in this text, I've introduced some common formatting errors into the dataset by combining the two tables included in the Excel workbook.

> **note**
>
> We discussed Tableau's separate prep tool offering, Tableau Prep, in a previous chapter. However, as Tableau Prep is a separate product, it is beyond the scope of this book. To learn more about Tableau Prep, visit ww.tableau.com/products/prep.

Data Interpreter in Action

Let's begin by connecting to the Significant Volcanic Eruptions dataset and drag out the "Volerup" sheet. As noted, I've introduced some simple formatting errors into this dataset to demonstrate the power of Data Interpreter. Now, although Tableau can easily connect to the data, the preview pane shows that some issues exist, including blank column names, nulls, and so on (Figure 8.1). Tableau has recognized these issues and suggests using Data Interpreter to help prepare the data for analysis.

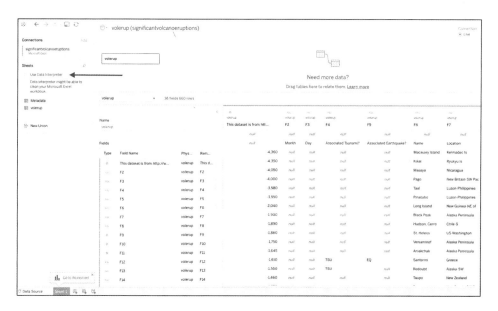

Figure 8.1 Although Tableau can connect to this messy data, some cleanup is still needed.

To "turn on" Data Interpreter, you need simply click the check box. Doing so will prompt Tableau to run the interpreter tool and the contents of the preview pane will update accordingly. You can see that those headers have been stripped out, and the columns are now properly identified (Figure 8.2).

Figure 8.2 With one click, Data Interpreter has helped prepare data for analysis.

There are still several issues to resolve in this dataset, but we can already see some improvement, as some blank rows have been removed from the preview and column names identified. To explore the specifics of what Data Interpreter has done to the data, you can click the blue Review the Results hyperlink. This will open an Excel file that includes a key describing the changes and that reflects the changes in individual sheets so you can efficiently identify work performed by Data Interpreter (Figure 8.3).

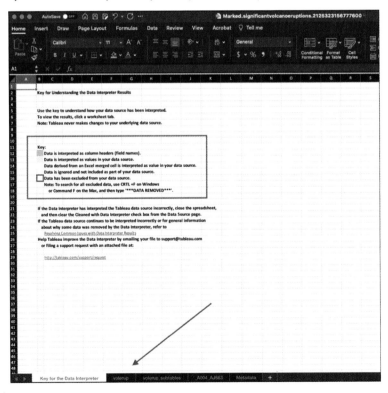

Figure 8.3 Data Interpreter provides a "marked" Excel workbook that details the changes made in the data.

> **note**
>
> Data Interpreter is not available if the data contains more than 2,000 columns or more than 3,000 rows *and* 150 columns. Likewise, this tool supports only Excel (.xls or .xlsx), Text (.csv), PDF, and Google Sheets files. If Tableau Desktop does not identify unique formatting issues or extraneous information that Data Interpreter is designed to adjust, the option will not be available.

If you click through the sheets, you can see which fields are being used as headers, in orange, and which are considered data, in green (Figure 8.4).

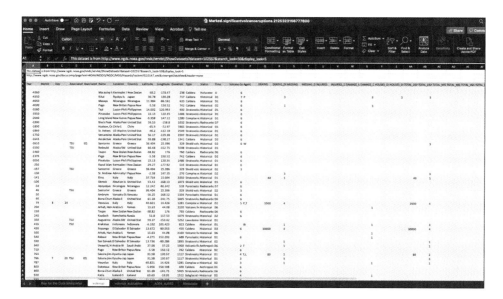

Figure 8.4 The data is color coded in the marked file.

Handling Nulls in Tableau

For this sample dataset, Data Interpreter has handled a good portion of the basic clean-up for us. However, before moving forward with this dataset, we need to resolve the nulls shown in the preview pane. The handling of nulls in Tableau is a dynamic and important step in the analysis process because null values—and how they are or are not used—can have a significant effect on the quality of your analytical work and visual outputs.

A null value is a field that is blank and signifies missing or unknown values. When a measure contains null values, they are usually plotted as zero. However, doing so can affect the analysis if these values are meant to be blank, or not applicable, rather than numerically quantified at zero. Depending on the reason for the null values, you may want to count them as zero, or perhaps you would rather suppress (hide) null values altogether. A variety of functions in Tableau work with null values:

- **IFNULL functions:** Perform a true/false test to determine whether the value in the tested field is null. The first value in the function is used if the value is not null, and the second is used if it is null.
- **ISNULL functions:** Test whether an expression is null (TRUE) or not (FALSE).
- **IIF functions:** Create a shorthand function for an IF-THEN-ELSE statement with the added benefit of defining a value if the test yields an unknown result.
- **ZN function:** A variation on the ISNULL and IFNULL functions; tests whether a function is null, and if it is, returns a value of zero.

Table 8.1 displays some of the different ways you can handle null values in Tableau. More training on handling nulls is available on the Tableau website.

Table 8.1 Key of Tableau functions for handling nulls.

Function	Explanation	Formula
Numeric Values		
ISNULL	Tests the numerical columns, and then gives output as "True" or "False"	IF ISNULL ([Measure]) THEN 0 ELSE [Measure] END
IFNULL	Tests the data, and then if a value is null, replaces it with the desired value (in this example, with 0)	IFNULL ([Measure], 0)
ZN	Tests the data and replaces nulls with 0	ZN([Measure])
IIF	Tests the data, and if null is found, replaces it with the desired value (0)	(IIF(IS NULL([Measure]), 0, [Measure]))
String Data		
ISNULL	Tests the data, and if nulls are found, replaces them with the desired string value	IF ISNULL([Dimension]) THEN "This is desired string value" ELSE [Dimension]
IFNULL	Test the data, and if nulls are found, replaces them with the desired string value	IFNULL([Dimension], "This record is null")
IIF	Tests the data, and if nulls are found, replaces them with the desired string value	IIF(ISNULL([Dimension]), "This record is Null," [Dimension])

WORKBOOK OPTIMIZER

A recent addition to Tableau's guided analytics and data literacy portfolio is Workbook Optimizer. Tableau's Workbook Organizer is a tool designed to identify whether a workbook follows certain performance best practices. These guidelines—which contain a "consider" statement that suggests potential ways to address the performance impact—are general in nature, and limited to what can be parsed from a workbook's metadata by a rules engine algorithm. Although not all recommendations are applicable for every workbook, this is a fantastic tool for ensuring your workbook is optimized before sharing it with your intended audience (Figure 8.5).

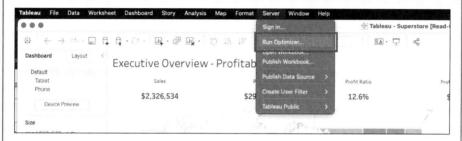

Figure 8.5 Tableau's new Workbook Optimizer identifies areas that can be improved according to established best practices.

The Workbook Optimizer breaks its guidelines down into three categories: take action, needs review, and passed.

- **Take action** items identify employable best practices that have minimal to no impact on workbook functionality and should usually be addressed.

- **Needs review** items may involve modifying the workbook in ways that affect workbook functionality (e.g., restructuring a data source).

- **Passed** indicates that guidelines are met, and best practices observed. If any guidelines have been ignored, this category is renamed **Passed and Ignored**.

> note
>
> There is much to discover and learn about Workbook Optimizer. Further information is available at https://help.tableau.com/current/pro/desktop/en-us/wbo_overview.htm.

Pivoting Data from Wide to Tall

A very common data prep task is to transform data from "wide"—meaning many, many columns—to "tall" (or "narrow")—meaning many, many rows. The difference lies in readability: Entering data into a spreadsheet in the wide form is generally easier for human comprehension, but computers prefer to read data in the tall form. In this regard, Tableau is similar. Reading "tall" data is preferable within the Tableau environment for use in visual analysis as well as for building and sorting charts dynamically.

A good example of wide versus tall data is survey data, which is, by nature, very wide. As an example, Figure 8.6 shows a raw export of survey data we'll return to later in this book.

> note
>
> This data was collected for a presentation at the Sixth Annual *Harry Potter* Conference hosted by Chestnut Hill College in Philadelphia. We'll return to this dataset to build data visualization and stories in later chapters. You can view the original presentation or learn more at HarryPotterConference.com.

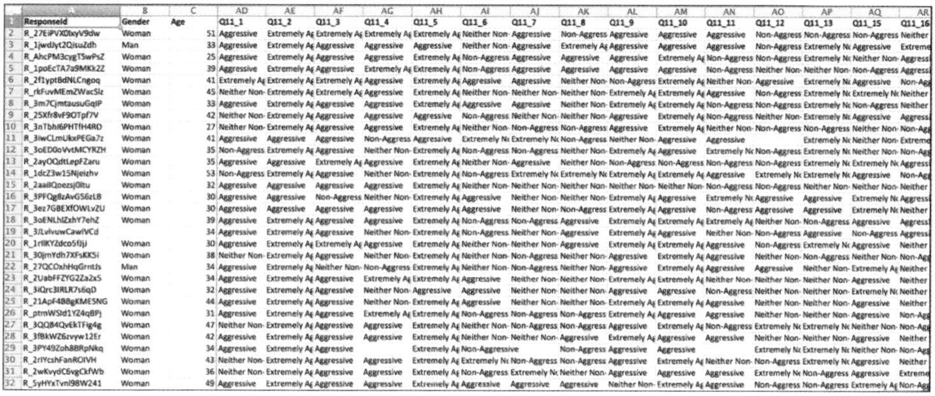

Figure 8.6 This raw survey data has been cleaned to remove extraneous formatting, but retains its original "wide" format when presented in Excel.

Here, each respondent's (listed in Column A) answers to each question are captured in one row, with each question in a separate column, resulting in many, many columns and very "wide" data. However, when analyzing survey data, you are interested in a respondent's answers, not the respondents themselves. Thus, you need the survey data to be tall so that you need to see every question's answer from every respondent, as opposed to every respondent's answer to every question. Reshaping survey data to be tall enables you to look at each question and distributes each respondent's answers to each question over many rows. Although this transformation can be done in Excel, pivoting data in Tableau is a matter of a few simple clicks.

In the following example, I have connected to a slightly modified version of the raw data presented in Figure 8.7. There's still some prep work to be done to get this data in shape for analysis, but you'll notice that each respondent's survey responses are contained in a single row and many columns, Q4, Q5, Q6, and so on (Figure 8.7). The first few columns contain demographic information related to each respondent.

To analyze this survey data, we need to reshape it from "wide" to "tall" before we can look at it meaningfully within Tableau. This can be achieved by using the Pivot function.

To pivot data in Tableau, select the columns that you would like to pivot, then use the drop-down menu to select the Pivot function. In this example, I would like to pivot each respondent's question answers against their basic demographic data, so I have selected all Question columns in Figure 8.8. You may select multiple fields to pivot by using the Shift key to highlight each column to be included in the function.

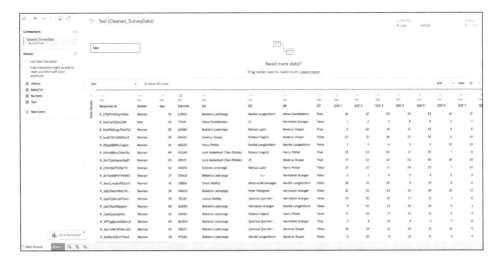

Figure 8.7 Imported into Tableau, this survey data has been cleaned to remove extraneous formatting but retains its original "wide" format.

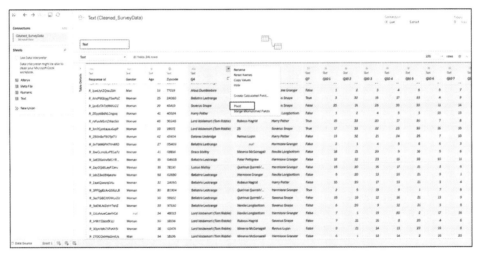

Figure 8.8 Using the Pivot function to reshape data from "wide" to "tall."

The result has given us "tall" data with two new columns—Pivot Field Names and Pivot Field Values, which contain the former columns and their respective data (Figure 8.9).

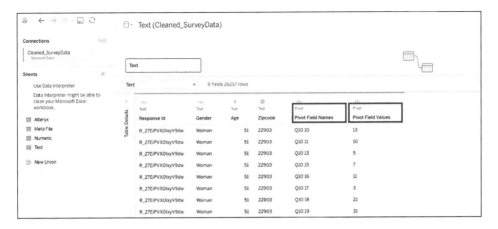

Figure 8.9 The Pivot function reshapes data, resulting in two new columns.

From here, we can simply use the Rename function (also available on the columns'
drop-down menu) to rename our columns to something more appropriate (Figure 8.9).
Now we are ready to begin our analysis.

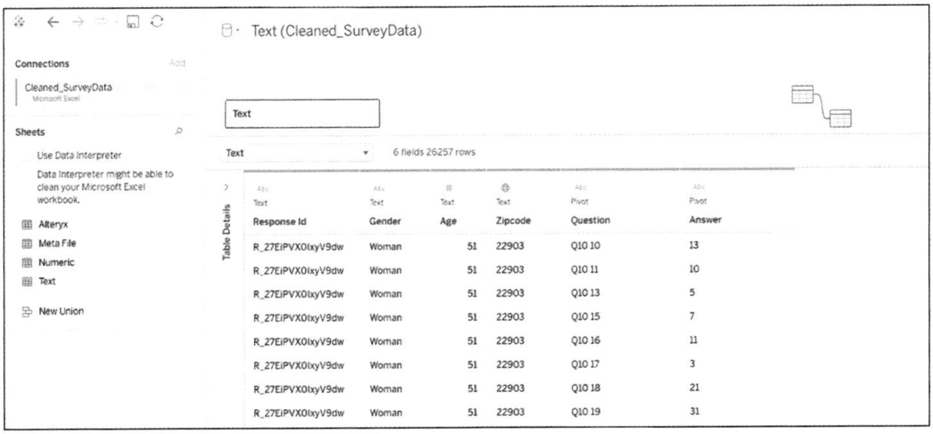

Figure 8.10 Rename pivot fields to make the new columns more meaningful.

A Note on Preparing Survey Data for Visual Analysis

Working with survey data is a common task in analytics. Preparing this type of data for analysis typically requires a hefty amount of manual work, in addition to more robust preparation tasks than can be achieved with Data Interpreter. Without extensive cleanup, analyzing raw survey data exported from tools such as SurveyMonkey or Qualtrics can be near impossible, both because of the usual formatting issues and because of the need to translate textual data into a format usable in analysis while preserving its metadata.

Survey data includes four elements you need to organize and fit together:

- Demographic information
- Responses in text form
- Responses in numeric form
- A "metafile" that acts as a legend to describe the survey

The goal is to combine all of these elements into a single, comprehensive view of the data—a tedious task.

While we won't embark on this prep process within the scope of this book, a word of caution is necessary here that applies to any data being used for analysis. There is truth to the old adage "Garbage in, garbage out." Before you begin preparing your data for analysis, you should spend time reviewing the data, even in its messiest raw form, and tidying up any errors or issues you see before you take further steps. In particular, look over and confirm date and geographic data formats, remove duplicate records, and change or correct any identifiers to the format that you need (e.g., capitalization). Fields that allow for manual text entry are especially prone to the latter issues, which might require your attention before you begin working with your data. This is also a perfect time to assess the presence of nulls in your data and determine when a field should be a null or a zero.

TEXT *AND* NUMERIC?

A keen observer might have noticed that the data in the figures used within this chapter thus far contains question fields that include both text and numeric responses, and that both are included in the list of survey data elements that should be combined for analysis. This may lead you to wonder why you want *both* text and numeric responses for the same question. The answer is simple. Most surveys include questions that ask respondents to select a value for a question.

Consider a question that asks for responses using a Likert scale, with the universe of possible values being indicated on a one-to-five (more common) or one-to-seven (less common) scale. For example, a survey Likert-scale question might be asked using the following format: "On a scale of 1 to 5, with 1 being 'extremely dissatisfied' and 5 being 'extremely satisfied,' how would you rank your dining experience?" These numeric values could also be given as a range such as "strongly agree to strongly disagree" or "extremely unimportant to extremely important." If you didn't allow for both numeric and text results, you would have to write a lot of IF/CASE statements and add unnecessary burden to the analytic process. We'll see this in action when we look at Likert charts as a type of advanced data visualization in a later chapter.

Among its many additions and improvements, Tableau v10 brought analysts the ability to prepare survey data without having to use external tools or spend countless hours engaged in a manual cleaning process. Keeping this process bundled within Tableau provides many benefits:

- It lessens overhead costs to invest in additional tools.
- It reduces the need to learn multiple pieces of software.
- It enables you to join created data sources directly within Tableau.

That said, there are also some drawbacks of this approach:

- The process is clunky and not intuitive.
- Tableau exhibits some strange behavior that necessitates users to repeat some steps.
- Users might need to create and routinely extract data.

note

Tableau Zen Master and Iron Viz Champion Steve Wexler maintains an excellent blog on reshaping survey data for Tableau, including using Excel, Tableau 10+, and Alteryx. His work includes many clearly delivered tutorials and presentations specifically on survey data and is an excellent resource. Visit Steve's blog at www.datarevelations.com/surveyjustso.html.

Whether you're working with survey data or any other dataset, once your data is properly cleaned and shaped, you're ready to begin visually exploring the data and creating visuals to tell its story. We've already worked together to build some fundamental data visualizations. Next, let's look at how to leverage these visuals to share with your audience in Tableau dashboards and stories.

Storyboarding Your Visual Analytics

Once your data has been thoroughly prepared for analysis and you've had the opportunity to spend some time visually experimenting with ways to explore and explain your insights through the basic visualizations, you're ready to construct a data narrative. This involves organizing the results of your analysis either by arranging them into visual data dashboards or by sequencing them to unfold into a compelling data story.

In an August 2017 episode of *The Nerdist* podcast, celebrated American astrophysicist (and phenomenal data storyteller) Neil DeGrasse Tyson spoke of the importance of learning how to process and understand today's firehose of information. He commented, "[We need to understand] how to turn data into information, information into knowledge, and knowledge into wisdom." In my opinion, this is exactly what we are doing when we build visual data stories.

Let's look at two primary storytelling capabilities available in Tableau: dashboards and stories. Proper dashboard design and a full review of Tableau features are well beyond the scope of this book, but we'll review fundamental best practices for utilizing both. From there, we'll discuss the steps you should take to build the appropriate framework for your narrative with a brief storytelling checklist.

> **note**
>
> You can build stories using Tableau sheets (individual visualizations), dashboards (multiple visualizations), or story points (multiple sheets and/or dashboards). Which mechanism you pick is up to you and is dependent on the needs of your audience, your delivery format, your presentation style, and other context. Overloading a dashboard is a real concern, particularly in non-narrated or guided presentations, as is trying to cram too much detail into a single visual or a story. In this chapter, we approach storyboarding from the perspective of building a narrative rather than formatting a delivery system. That said, the chapter does cover a few basic aspects of working with dashboards and stories that support your storytelling process.

Understanding Stories in Tableau

Earlier chapters distilled the difference between exploratory and explanatory visualizations, and the obligation of visual analysts and data storytellers to focus on building and sharing visualizations that support the story. Like events in any narrative, visualizations should compound on each other and lead the audience through a series of events, insights, or other information that allows them to reach the goal you have decided on upfront.

Building stories in Tableau relies on three primary mechanisms: sheets, dashboards, and stories (called story points in Tableau).

best practice

Although all three of these mechanisms can support great visual data stories, be strategic in how you use them. Be aware of the impact of sizing, layout, and positioning, and make sure the view you've curated on your screen is consistent with your audience's. The Device Preview functionality in Tableau supports this practice.

Individual Visualizations (Sheets)

Sometimes one visual is all you need, particularly if it is layered with rich tooltips or annotations. Or, you might want to export simple, static visuals for use in other presentation software. So far, we've spent our time applying fundamental visual analysis principles within the sheets—or canvas—environment in Tableau. From here, you can bring individual visualizations into dashboards or story points to build a storytelling framework. A sheet is the building block for any story, as it is the place where visualizations are built.

note

Many analysts use PowerPoint to present visualizations, but this requires exporting static images of your visuals, instead of letting them stay within their native format and keep any interactive functionality. Instead of this approach, try Tableau Reader, which is a simple, free download that lets everyone appreciate Tableau views at their best, including the ability to "touch" your data as you present it. Additionally, views can be shared to Tableau Public.

Dashboards

A dashboard is a collection of several worksheets shown in a single screen so that you can compare and monitor a variety of data visualizations simultaneously. It often offers the ability to filter and highlight all visualizations through a single dashboard action. Dashboards, like visualizations, can achieve many purposes, and can be designed to explain, explore, or tell stories. Storytelling dashboards seek to weave together a series of visuals that show how something unfolds and should be aligned with the narrative flow.

You can create a dashboard in Tableau by clicking the Dashboard button at the bottom of the Tableau workspace (Figure 8.11).

Figure 8.11 Dashboard button.

In terms of a delivery mechanism for visual analysis, as with visualizations. you can create several types of dashboards—explanatory, exploratory, and so on. Like individual visualizations, dashboards can be approached as either analytical or storytelling in nature. Storytelling dashboards tend to have the following characteristics:

- Have more descriptive titles and lead-in paragraphs, often including legends (based on color or size) within their design.
- Have simplified and streamlined views of a smaller number of visualizations.
- Include prominent legends, simplified color schemes, and limited views of data, including only those that support the narrative (that is, filters or parameters).
- Omit interactive elements that might affect the narrative, such as quick filters or other actions (this often depends on whether the presentation will be narrated or left to the audience).
- Include explanatory annotations to point out specific "story points" the narrator deems of interest to the audience.

Figure 8.12 shows an example of a simple dashboard using some of the visuals we created earlier in this book.

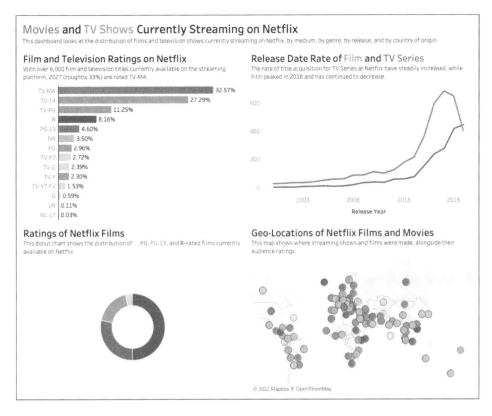

Figure 8.12 A simple dashboard.

Visual Hierarchy

You might have noticed that both Tableau's Dashboard and the dashboard presented in Figure 8.12 follow a four-quadrant approach. This format creates a visual hierarchy—that is, an arrangement or presentation of elements in a way that implies importance. In other words, visual hierarchy influences the order in which the human eye perceives what it sees—left to right, top to bottom. This order is created by the visual contrast between forms in a field of perception.

While dashboards are certainly not limited to this quadrant approach, it is considered best practice. The arrangement of visuals within the quadrant space should likewise be organized in a way to make the most of how the human brain intrinsically organizes information in terms of importance.

- **Top left:** This should be the most important visualization on the dashboard.
- **Top right:** This space is reserved for the second most important visualization. If there's no obvious hierarchy between the second and third visualizations, time series graphs are a good option to fill this space.

- ■ **Bottom left:** This is neutral territory, for visualizations of lesser importance.

- ■ **Bottom right:** This is the area of least emphasis. Maps, because they are encoded with location information that makes them easy to read without much energy expenditure but typically provide less analytical value, are great candidates for this space.

The overlay presented in Figure 8.13 shows how the dashboard in Figure 8.12 aligns to the four-quadrant best-practice approach.

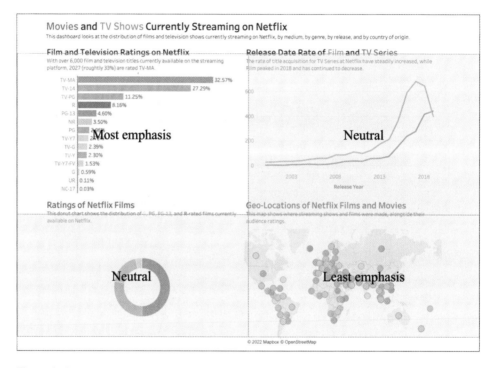

Figure 8.13 A simple dashboard with a four-quadrant overlay for visual hierarchy.

THE DASHBOARD WORKSPACE

Many of the formatting features of Tableau sheets apply intuitively to dashboards. Figure 8.14 presents an annotated view of the Tableau dashboard workspace so that we can take a look at some of the additional functionality features available.

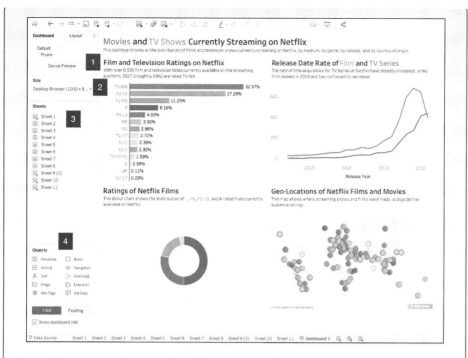

Figure 8.14 An annotated view of the Tableau dashboard workspace.

1. **Device Preview:** This option allows you to see your dashboard as it will appear on the form factor selected in Size.

2. **Size:** This is an important aspect to think about *before* you start building a dashboard, and these options let you select from a preprogrammed list of fixed display sizes (that is, desktop browser, laptop browser, tablet) while the canvas adjusts accordingly. The Automatic option allows the dashboard display to dynamically resize to any display on which it is presented, but this choice has certain ramifications for things like floating legends, which will move around as the screen resizes.

3. **Sheets:** This area lists all sheets in the workbook.

4. **Objects:** This area lists additional elements, such as logos and images, that you may elect to add into your dashboard from outside of Tableau.

note

This section provides only a very basic overview of dashboard functionality. You can find more information on creating a dashboard, including adding views, objects, and interactivity, at www.tableau.com/learn/get-started/dashboards.

Story Points

Story points were introduced in Tableau version 8.2 as a way to "build a narrative from data." Tableau Story Points is similar to other presentation software in it enables a presenter to highlight certain insights or provide content, as well as break the story into pieces using visualizations (whether as worksheets or dashboards) in a series of click-through sequences for easy consumption. A story is a sheet, so the same methods you would apply to create, name, and manage visualizations in worksheets also apply to stories.

The benefit to using Tableau Story Points, rather than using PowerPoint or similar, is that with it, interactivity remains in the story. Story points are not static images: Presenters or audiences can explore or expand on the data using actions such as quick filters within the narrative. Additionally, Tableau Story Points updates in real time as the underlying visualizations or data is updated, reducing the need for reworking or re-exporting worksheets.

You can create a story in Tableau by clicking the Story button (Figure 8.15).

Figure 8.15 Story button.

You present stories by clicking the Presentation Mode button (Figure 8.16) on the toolbar.

Figure 8.16 Presentation Mode button.

Figure 8.17 shows an example of Tableau Story Points in action using presentation mode.

> **note**
>
> To find more information on creating a story, including layout options, formatting, and presentation, go to https://help.tableau.com/current/pro/ desktop/en-us/stories.htm.

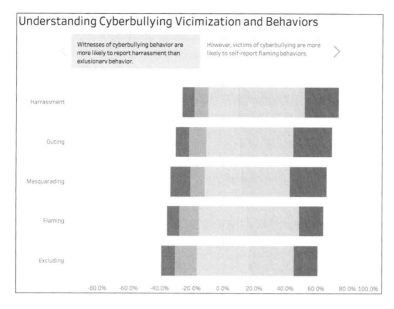

Figure 8.17 Story Points in presentation mode.

THE STORY POINTS WORKSPACE

Many of the formatting features of Tableau sheets and dashboards apply intuitively to stories. Figure 8.18 presents an annotated view of the Tableau Story Points workspace so that we can take a look at some of the additional functionality features available.

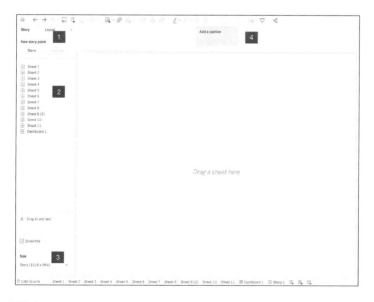

Figure 8.18 An annotated view of the Tableau Story Points workspace.

1. **New story point:** You may insert a blank or duplicate a story point.

2. **Story pane:** This box contains all the worksheets and dashboards in your workbook that can be added as a story point.

3. **Size:** Again, size is important. This option lets you resize your storytelling canvas.

4. **Captions/navigation:** Captions, similar in concept to annotations, provide a tool to "narrate" your story. These can be formatted to include text, be numbered, or utilize advancement dots or arrows (Figure 8.19)

The Layout pane provides further options intended to help you format the style of navigation for the text boxes. Navigation can be formatted as caption boxes (default), numbered, arrows, or dots (Figure 8.19).

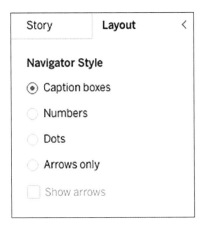

Figure 8.19 Format navigation in the Layout pane within Tableau Story Points.

THE STORYTELLING CHECKLIST

Before building a story, make sure to complete this Storytelling Checklist and answer as many questions as possible before moving into the storyboarding process to ensure the story aligns to your goals. You can then start sketching the story outline for guidance during development of the narrative. We'll take a look at some data storytelling best practices in Chapter 10.

- **Who: The Data's Audience**
  - Who is your audience?
  - What do they want?

- What do they need?

- How might they be feeling?

- What action do they need to take?

- What type of communication do they prefer?

- How well do they know the data?

- **You**

  - How well does the audience know you?

  - Does the audience trust you? Do they find you credible?

  - How well do you know the data?

  - Do you have any preconceived notions or bias about the data?

- **What: The Data's Context**

  - What is the data?

  - What is it about? Is the data complete?

  - Do you have enough data to tell a complete story?

  - Is the subject matter general or specialized?

- **Why: The Goal**

  - Why are you telling this story?

  - What action do you want the audience to take?

- **How: The Data's Presentation Mode**

  - Is this story static or interactive?

  - Will you be narrating the story?

  - Do you want to explore or expand the story while narrating?

  - Will it be presented in a small group or a large setting?

  - Will the audience be live or virtual?

The Storyboarding Process

Like all aspects of data visualization, crafting a perfect visual data story is a process of ongoing iteration and refinement. Luckily, crafting a data story is much like crafting any other narrative. After taking the time to clean and explore your data, you can take advantage of a rather linear process to build a complete visual data story (Figure 8.20).

Figure 8.20 This linear process can help you craft the best visual data narrative.

Planning Your Story's Purpose

Whichever mechanism you are using, as you begin planning your story, taking some time to reflect on the purpose of the story and the narrative you want to share with your captivated audience is critical. Defining this purpose is the single most important step of the planning stage in the storytelling.

We discussed the seven types of data stories in an earlier chapter. Pick one. **ONE**. Regardless of the type of story you are telling, your story should have one goal, and one goal only. The clarity of your story is just as important as the clarity of each visualization within it. Audiences shouldn't have to guess to understand the salient point you are trying to make with your presentation.

In addition to the Storytelling Checklist, think like an author and consider the following aspects of your narrative:

- **Plot:** What story are you trying to tell? What is its purpose, and what is your goal or the action you want the audience to take when you roll the credits, figuratively speaking, at the end of your story?

- **Characters:** Think of your data as your main character, and its context as the story's setting. Your filters, parameters, limitations, and even external data sources are all supporting characters in your story, and each contributes to the overall narrative. It's your job to identify how.

- **Audience:** Consider each of the questions in the Storytelling Checklist. Like any good storyteller, you should know who is going to be listening to or reading your story.

Storyboarding Your Data Story

As you begin constructing your story, considering order and flow and how the pieces of your story fit together is important. You've already seen the importance of understanding the data's context and of audience analysis and how the story's purpose is supported by understanding its plot, characters, and audience. You've also reviewed several common types of data visualizations and know how to curate them to make them more intuitive, focused, and compelling. Your story will, when complete, tie together all of these elements into a cohesive whole.

Stories may be composed of various views of a single visualization, of a series of compounding similar visualizations, or of a series of unique visualizations that support different aspects of an analysis. There is no single correct way to build a story. The example in this chapter tells a story about survey data, and in doing so shows how to work through a series of unique visualizations that support the story structure and take advantage of several chart types explored in this book.

Although many different types of narrative structures exist and are worthy of consideration, the one I have found most effective for consistently telling compelling, meaningful visual data stories regardless of the type of story is the three-act structure. Let's review how this structure functions:

- **Act One—The Setup (or, the Exposition):** This is where you, as the narrator, lay the groundwork for your story. It's where you explain the purpose, introduce the plot, establish the characters and their relationships, and finish with your dramatic question or inciting incident. This is the catalyst; it's the type of story you are telling. Are you going to explore a change over time? Zoom into detail on something that happened? Act One ends with your hypothesis, or what question you are exploring or answering within your story.

- **Act Two—The Rising Action:** This is the meat of your story. It's where you combine plot, characters, and audience as you guide them through the data. In a film or play, Act Two typically depicts a protagonist's attempt to resolve a problem or the escalation of an issue, and who experiences character development along the way. In a visual data narrative, this is your opportunity to perform a curated version of your own analysis, capitalizing on the insights you have found that support your narrative's purpose—and making your audience believe in your discoveries as they experience the story for themselves.

- **Act Three—The Climax:** Finally, you've reached your grand reveal. Your audience has absorbed the plot point and is ready for their call to action via a final viz that ends the story.

> **note**
>
> You can use many techniques to build your storyboard. One of the most common (and the one I use in my classroom) is the sticky note approach. This process involves using color-coded sticky notes (yellow for Act One, pink for Act Two, green for Act Three) and treating each sticky note as a view in your story. You can easily adjust and rearrange your storyboard based on audience feedback and as you fine-tune the visuals and supporting narrative.

Summary

Building dashboards and stories as mechanisms to share the results of visual data analysis is a topic worthy of further research and exploration. I've provided a list of recommended reading in Chapter 10 and other educational resources in the Appendix to support your ongoing learning. Now, with the basics behind us, let's take a look at a few of the advanced visualizations Tableau can support for your work with visual analytics.

CHAPTER 9

BEYOND FUNDAMENTALS: ADVANCED VISUALIZATIONS

This penultimate chapter explores advanced strategies that go beyond fundamental data visualizations and explore a curated subset of advanced data visualizations that go beyond the Tableau Show Me card. We'll cover how to create advanced charts that require additional formatting and calculations, including timelines, Likert-scale charts, lollipop charts, and more.

As discussed in Chapters 5 and 6, you can create many fundamental data visualizations by using the menu of charts presented in the Show Me card. These require little manual formatting other than tidying up the visualizations and cover the chart types most commonly used in visual analytics.

This chapter goes beyond these basic options and takes a look at how to create several advanced charts, step by step, in Tableau. These charts, which are only a fraction of the advanced visualizations that can be created by the savvy visual analyst in Tableau, are readily accessible to emerging learners, as they require little more than the use of calculated fields and additional formatting to build. However, these advanced visualizations offer deeper, more dynamic views into data and can be beneficial in supporting more complex analytics. The advanced visualizations covered in this chapter are

- Timelines
- Bar-in-bar charts
- Likert-scale visualizations
- Lollipop charts
- Word clouds

Timelines

A timeline can be a useful way to depict events that occur over time, whether the goal is analyzing patterns in notable events or showing dates of interest. Although a timeline isn't a graph that can be built out of the box in Tableau, you can create one by following a few simple steps. The resulting visual can support storytelling when you're discussing important events over time (Figure 9.1).

Creating this visualization requires a very simple dataset. At minimum, you need only two pieces of information: a date and an event. Additional detail, such as location or event type, can help enhance a basic timeline and yield something even more exciting and visually engaging.

For this exercise, I have connected to a small, simple Excel dataset of horror movie heroines, titled "Final Girls." This set includes the name of the character, the film in which she appeared, and the release date of the film, as well as some general notes (Figure 9.2). Because this is a working dataset, I've used Data Interpreter to help tidy the data and performed a few manual tweaks to prepare it for analysis.

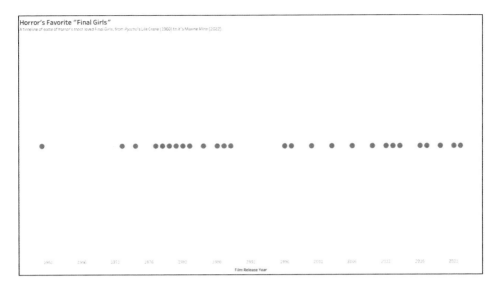

Figure 9.1 A snapshot of a finished visual timeline.

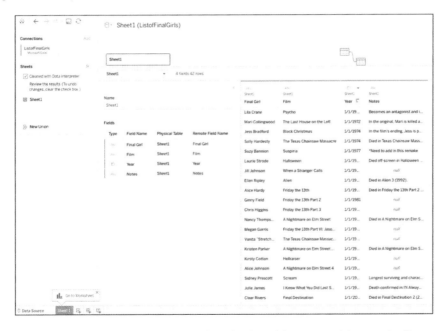

Figure 9.2 A simple timeline requires minimal data: the date of the event and the event itself.

<blockquote>

note

For this timeline, we're using a dataset of "final girls" depicted in horror movies over time. The dataset is available for download on the companion website to this text.

</blockquote>

Before beginning, in your sheet, make sure that your date is recognized by Tableau as a *continuous* date. If it is not, you can change it by right-clicking the field on the Dimensions pane, and selecting Convert to Continuous on the list of options (Figure 9.3).

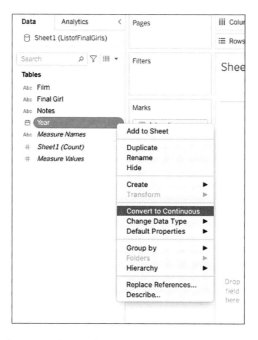

Figure 9.3 Adjust your date to continuous if it is not already. This allows you to view an event over a span of time, rather than in isolation.

The key to constructing a timeline in Tableau is to create a calculated field that will form the horizontal axis of the timeline and allow all of your dates to line up on a straight line. Think of this field as an anchor to hold your events to time. Create the Anchor calculated field by following these steps:

1. Right-click the Data pane and create a new calculated field called Anchor. The field should contain the input MIN(0), as shown in Figure 9.4.

2. Drag the newly created Anchor calculated field to the Rows shelf to provide a starting point for your timeline. At this point, your visualization is simply a horizontal axis line with a zero line (Figure 9.5).

Figure 9.4 Create a simple calculated field to "anchor" your horizontal timeline.

Figure 9.5 The Anchor placeholder gives a straight axis to begin plotting your events.

3. Drag your Date field to the Columns shelf. Right-click the Date pill and select Exact Date. This prompts Tableau to recognize each of the exact dates listed in your dataset of events and lays the foundation of the timeline by displaying a flat, solid, colored line (Figure 9.6). Because there is no additional data, this is correct.

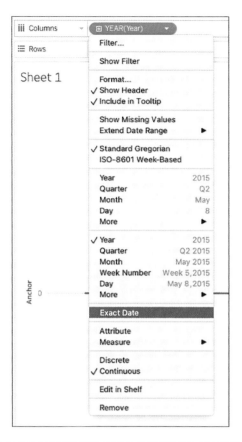

Figure 9.6 Adding the Date field to the Columns shelf provides the foundation of a timeline.

note

Calculated fields enable you to extend your analysis by creating a new field (or column) that is not already contained in your data source. To create a new calculated field, in a Tableau worksheet, select Analysis > Create Calculated Field. The Calculation Editor dialog box will open, which prompts you to give the calculated field a name and provide a formula. Formulas can be created using a combination of functions, fields, and operators. Once created, the new calculated field will appear as a new measure in the Data pane and be designated with an equal (=) sign that precedes the field name.

With the baseline set, you can now add dated events and begin formatting the timeline to look more traditional. To do so, drag the Date dimension from the Data pane again, and this time drop it on the Details Marks card. Initially, the timeline may continue to appear flat. This is because Tableau automatically looks at the largest segment of the date—in this case, Year.

Depending on the level of detail in your date data hierarchy, you may need to prompt Tableau to look at a more granular view of the date. Do this by clicking the + icon on the pill to expand the date to the level you'd prefer to see on the timeline. Your timeline should now display each of the events in your dataset as individual dots (Figure 9.7).

Figure 9.7 With event dates added to the baseline, the timeline begins to take form.

A bit of additional formatting can enable this timeline to tell a more detailed story about the events displayed. You might use color to distinguish event types, for example. The shape and size of each event point can be enlarged, and a tooltip added to provide more information (Figure 9.8). You can also adjust or delete zero lines, axis rules, and axis ticks as desired.

Figure 9.8 A little bit of additional formatting can add more detail and visual impact to your timeline.

Here are a few additional things you can do to spice up a timeline and make it more visually appealing:

- **Add a time frame.** When you have a large number of events to display, adding a relative date filter to show only the events within a certain span of time might be helpful. To do this, drag the Date dimension to the Filters shelf and choose Relative Dates. You can set the logic to be any subset of dates that you want to dynamically display. In this example, I have limited the range to a mere 30 days (Figure 9.9).

Figure 9.9 Filter the dates in a view to limit the number of events displayed.

- **Add a reference line for "Today."** A reference line for the current date can give audiences a visual checkpoint on the timeline. To create a reference line, follow these steps:

  1. Create a new calculated field, Today: TODAY().

  2. Place this newly created calculated field on the Details Marks card. This allows the field to be used as a reference line. Adjust the field from a discrete date by right-clicking the date pill and selecting Exact Date.

  3. To add the reference line onto the timeline, select Reference Line from the Analytics pane. Choose the Today calculated field as the Line Value for the line and set it at Minimum (Figure 9.10).

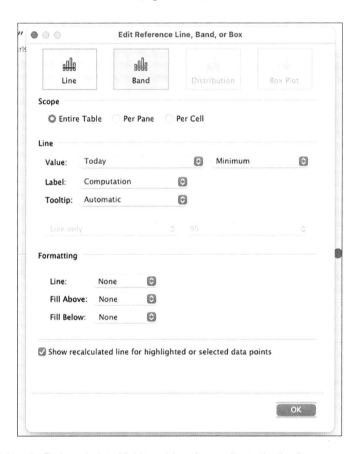

Figure 9.10 Use the Today calculated field to add a reference line to the timeline.

The Line Label option Custom enables you to specify how the line will be labeled on the canvas. Further formatting can also be completed in this box to define how you want the line to visually appear.

> note
>
> Timelines are a great visualization type with which to experiment with custom shapes. Refer to Chapter 7 to learn more about custom shapes and how to use them, or visit www.tableau.com/drive/custom-shapes.

With a few formatting tweaks, you can finalize a visually appealing timeline that makes a great asset to a dashboard or data story.

Bar-in-Bar Charts

We looked at several forms of basic bar charts in Chapter 5, including side-by-side and stacked bar charts. Both of these options are available out of the box in Tableau. However, quantitative comparison may become difficult with stacked bar charts when the stacks pile on top of one another, rather than starting at a baseline of zero. In such a case, a better option in the bar chart landscape is a bar-in-bar chart. These charts can be useful when comparing a measure against a goal or comparing two measures (or discrete dimensions) against each other, with both items starting at the zero line for a precise analysis (Figure 9.11).

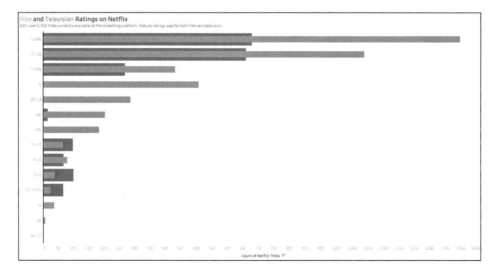

Figure 9.11 This bar-in-bar chart takes a stacked bar chart to the next level by adding data while preserving quantitative value.

Building a bar-in-bar chart in Tableau is not terribly difficult, but it does require taking a few additional manual steps to help get your bars in the shape you want. Like other bar charts, bar-in-bar charts can be created either horizontally or vertically. As our example here, we'll build a horizontal one.

The first step in building a bar-in-bar chart is to create a slightly odd-looking stacked bar chart by dragging one measure to the Rows shelf and one dimension to the Columns shelf (in our example I have filtered out unnecessary data, as seen on the Filter marks card). Next, drag your second dimension to the Color Marks card, and then drag this same dimension to the Size Marks card. You should see a stacked bar chart with dimensions differentiated by color and by size (Figure 9.12).

Figure 9.12 A bar-in-bar chart begins with a slightly odd-looking stacked bar chart.

At this point, the two dimensions are stacked together along the *x*-axis of the measure, rather than laid atop each other with both starting at the zero point. This stacking is an automatic function of Tableau that you need to turn off to manually build your bar-in-bar chart. To disable this feature, navigate to the Analysis menu and choose Stack Marks > Off (Figure 9.13).

After this step, you should have a raw version of your bar-in-bar chart. At this point, you can adjust which dimensions are in the foreground and the background by dragging and dropping to sort the measures on the Color Marks card filter, if desired. You can also edit the width of the bars by clicking the drop-down menu on the Size filter, selecting Edit Sizes, and then adjusting the Mark Size Range slider as desired (Figure 9.14). Complete your visualization by editing and removing axis headers, titles, sorting bars, and so on.

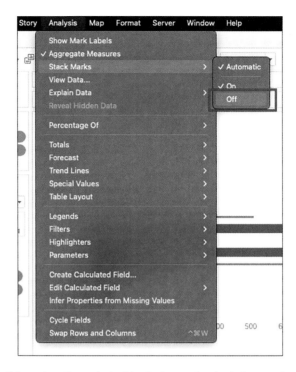

Figure 9.13 Turn off the automatic mark-stacking feature on the Analysis menu to overlay components of stacked bars.

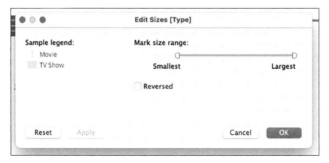

Figure 9.14 Adjust the width of the bars by editing the size range on the Size filter menu.

Continue to format your viz as desired to clean up and curate the bar-in-bar chart.

Likert-Scale Visualizations

Likert scales are the most widely used approach to scaling responses to gauge sentiment and tendencies, and they are a staple of surveys and other types of data collection methodologies. Likert-scale questions can be asked in several ways and, in turn, the data collected can be visualized in multiple ways. This section takes a closer look at the two most common Likert scales and the best ways to visualize them: a 100% stacked bar chart and a divergent bar chart.

Before discussing how to build Likert-scale visualizations, let's examine what Likert-scale data looks like. Figure 9.15 shows an example of a five-point Likert scale using an example from the Harry Potter dataset. On five-point Likert scales, values typically range from one extreme to another (for example, "highly satisfied" to "highly dissatisfied"), with a neutral option residing midrange.

On a Scale of 1 to 5, with 1 being Extremely Non-Aggressive and 5 being Extremely Aggressive, how would you rate each of the following Harry Potter characters?

	Extremely Non-Aggressive	Non-Aggressive	Neither Non-Aggressive Nor Aggressive	Aggressive	Extremely Aggressive
Harry Potter					
Hermione Granger					
Severus Snape					
Lord Voldemort					
Ron Weasley					

Figure 9.15 A five-point Likert scale.

Whereas five-point Likert scales are commonly used to measure sentiment, four-point Likert scales are more typically used to measure tendencies. Figure 9.16 shows an example of a four-point Likert scale using an example from the Cyberbullying dataset.

Have you ever enacted any of the following cyberbullying behaviors?

	Often	Sometimes	Just Once	Never
Posted Rude Comments				
Teased/Threatened Someone Online				
Hacked Into Someone's Account				
Used Information Found Online to Tease/Harass				
Posted Pictures of Someone Without Permission				

Figure 9.16 A four-point Likert scale.

> note
>
> When preparing Likert data for analysis, the recommendation is to have both a text value and a numerical value associated.

A 100% Stacked Bar Chart

A stacked bar chart is a simple, straightforward way to visualize data from Likert-scale questions that does not involve the creation of any calculated fields and requires little manual work (Figure 9.17).

Figure 9.17 A 100% stacked bar chart can be an easy way of visualizing Likert-scale data, although it falls short of the richness that other methods can add to the data's story.

To create the visualization in Figure 9.17, drag your first dimension to the Rows shelf (this example uses survey data, so the field is Wording) and a measure to the Columns shelf. A simple horizontal bar chart with solid-color bars of equal length, representing the total *count* of responses for each dimension, appears.

Next, drag your second dimension that represents the Answer value (or the value representing survey responses) to the Color Marks card (Figure 9.18).

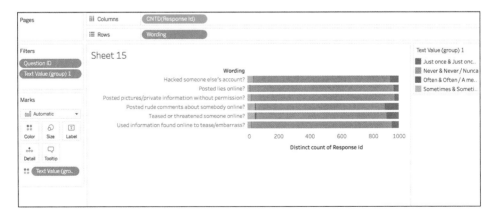

Figure 9.18 A rough stacked bar chart begins to visualize Likert-scale data; however, it requires more curation to be a truly useful visualization.

A number of things need to be done to improve this basic 100% stacked bar chart to properly visualize the Likert-scale data:

- **Color:** The default color scheme in Tableau does little to help us see behaviors that are adjacent to each other (for example, sometimes/often and just once/ never). Using the Color Marks card, adjust these to a more suitable color palette.

- **Sort:** Tendencies are sorted in alphabetical order rather than by how often they occur. Manually sort these data to reflect the correct order.

- **Totals:** A count of data is an okay option, but a better option (particularly in survey data) may be "percentage of total." Add in the correct table calculation to make this change.

- **Curate:** Remove unnecessary headers to clean up your canvas.

> note
>
> You can apply several types of calculations to transform the values for a measure in Tableau, including custom calculations, table calculations, level of detail (LOD) expressions, and more. For more information on the various types of calculations and how to use them, visit https://help.tableau.com/ current/pro/desktop/en-us/calculations_calculatedfields_understand_ types.htm.

With a bit of tweaking, this 100% stacked bar chart can be a decent approach to display Likert-scale responses (Figure 9.19). You could also add labels for each category to see the percentage of responses per tendency.

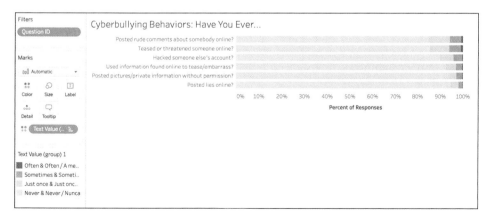

Figure 9.19 With better colors and sorting, this 100% stacked bar chart does a better job of visualizing the Likert-scale data.

Divergent Stacked Bar Chart

Although the 100% stacked bar chart will *work* to represent Likert-scale data, a better approach is a divergent bar chart—which is not actually a bar chart, but rather a modified version of a Gantt chart. Rather than stacking tendencies or sentiment ratings on a scale of 0 to 100, this approach shows the spread of negative and positive sentiment values (such as "strongly disagree" to "strongly agree") aligned to each other around the neutral midpoint (Figure 9.20).

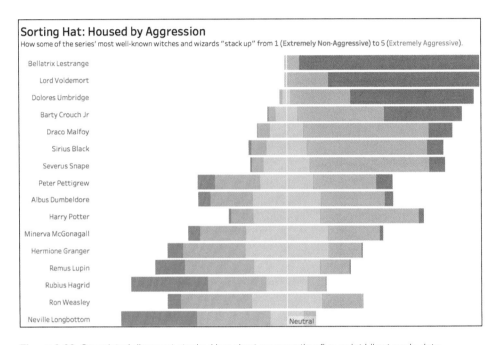

Figure 9.20 Completed divergent stacked bar chart representing five-point Likert-scale data.

This approach requires you to create several calculated fields. To begin building this visualization, you must first create a table, or crosstab, in Tableau. This enables you to see the output of each of the calculations you build and to troubleshoot any calculation errors before moving into visualizing them.

> **note**
>
> For this challenging chart, you will use the Harry Potter dataset used in previous chapters. Download the dataset to follow along with the steps.

In this table, first drag the QuestionID and Text Value dimensions to the Row shelf. (In this example, the QuestionID has been renamed to match the character name for readability.) Because we included both the text and the numeric coding for each Answer field, we can avoid writing any calculations at this point (the Numeric Value for each response will become useful in the next steps). However, notice that when you add this dimension, the Text Values are not in the sequence they should be. Click the drop-down menu on the Text Value dimension on the Rows shelf, select Sort, and manually adjust these values so that they display in the correct ranking order (minimum to maximum, or 1 to 5). Then, drop the Number of Records Measure (SUM) onto the Text Marks card. Your table should appear similar to Figure 9.21.

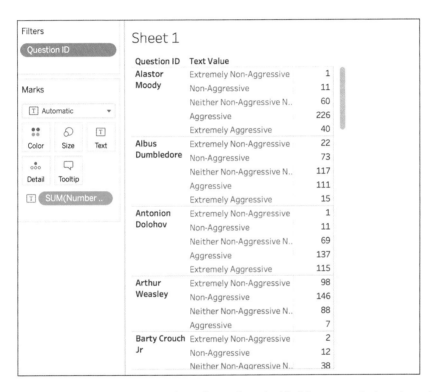

Figure 9.21 After this step, you can see for each question asked (in this case, each character ranked) how many respondents chose each option on the Likert scale.

The next step is to create a series of calculated fields and add them onto the table.

Calculated Field #1: Negative Sentiment

The first calculated field will calculate how many negative sentiment responses were received for each question (or item ranked); these data should appear as negative values and be positioned below (or to the left of) the dividing line of 0 in the divergent stacked bar chart. To do this, we need to count the number of responses received for the two lowest selections on the scale (in this case 1—extremely non-aggressive and 2—non-aggressive) as well as *half* of the neutral selection (in this case, 3—neither non-aggressive nor aggressive). Because neutral responses in a survey are neither positive nor negative, we want to split them in half to distribute them across the bars in the chart so as to not unfairly weight one side of the data.

Create this calculated field, named Negative Sentiment:

> IF [Numeric Value] < 3 THEN 1 ELSEIF [Numeric Value] = 3 THEN 0.5 ELSE 0 END

Add this calculation onto the canvas. Your screen should match that shown in Figure 9.22; the Number of Responses in the two negative sentiment ranks should match the count in the Negative Sentiment column. The neutral response count for Negative Sentiment should be half the count of Number of Responses, and the two positive sentiment ranks should appear with a count of 0 in the Negative Sentiment column.

Question ID	Text Value	Number of Records	Negative Sentiment
Alastor Moody	Extremely Non-Aggressive	1.0	1.0
	Non-Aggressive	11.0	11.0
	Neither Non-Aggressive N..	60.0	30.0
	Aggressive	226.0	0.0
	Extremely Aggressive	40.0	0.0
Albus Dumbledore	Extremely Non-Aggressive	22.0	22.0
	Non-Aggressive	73.0	73.0
	Neither Non-Aggressive N..	117.0	58.5
	Aggressive	111.0	0.0
	Extremely Aggressive	15.0	0.0

Figure 9.22 This calculated field counts the number of negative sentiment responses that will appear on the negative side of the dividing 0.

Calculated Field #2: Total Negative Sentiment

The next step is to create a calculated field to calculate the percentage of negative values per question. Create this calculated field, named Total Negative Sentiment:

> TOTAL(SUM([Negative Sentiment]))

This calculated field is a default table calculation; however, we need to manually change the field being used to compute the calculation. From within the calculated field editor box, click the blue text Default Table Calculation. Then select Text Value from the list (Figure 9.23).

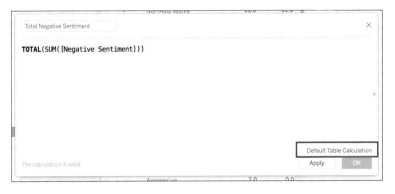

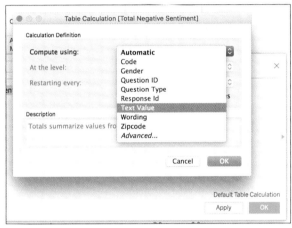

Figure 9.23 This calculated field calculates the percentage of negative values per question.

After you add this calculated field to your crosstab, it should resemble Figure 9.24. Notice that the Total Negative Sentiment value is the same for each QuestionID. This function simply sums the values in the Negative Sentiment column for each item scored. For example, Alastor Moody has a Negative Sentiment Count of 1 + 11 + 30 = 42. This total sentiment appears in the Total Negative Sentiment column.

Question ID	Text Value	Number of Records	Negative Sentiment	Total Negative Sentiment
Alastor Moody	Extremely Non-Aggressive	1.0	1.0	42.0
	Non-Aggressive	11.0	11.0	42.0
	Neither Non-Aggressive N..	60.0	30.0	42.0
	Aggressive	226.0	0.0	42.0
	Extremely Aggressive	40.0	0.0	42.0
Albus Dumbledore	Extremely Non-Aggressive	22.0	22.0	153.5
	Non-Aggressive	73.0	73.0	153.5
	Neither Non-Aggressive N..	117.0	58.5	153.5
	Aggressive	111.0	0.0	153.5
	Extremely Aggressive	15.0	0.0	153.5

Figure 9.24 The Total Negative Sentiment function sums the individual count of negative responses per question scored.

Calculated Field #3: Total Sentiment Scores

Now that we have the percentage of the total for the negative values, we need to find the percentage of the total for the entire bar and add up the responses for each item scored.

Create this calculated field, named Total Sentiment Scores:

TOTAL(SUM([Number of Records]))

You will need to change the default table calculation to Text Values.

When added to the crosstab, this calculated field will sum the number of responses per question. If your dataset is nice and clean and all questions were answered, the value in this column should be the same all the way down. For datasets in which not every question was answered, such as this one, you will see variations in the count of responses in this column (Figure 9.25).

Question ID	Text Value	Number of Records	Negative Sentiment	Total Negative Sentiment	Total Sentiment Scores
Alastor Moody	Extremely Non-Aggressive	1.0	1.0	42.0	338.0
	Non-Aggressive	11.0	11.0	42.0	338.0
	Neither Non-Aggressive N..	60.0	30.0	42.0	338.0
	Aggressive	226.0	0.0	42.0	338.0
	Extremely Aggressive	40.0	0.0	42.0	338.0
Albus Dumbledore	Extremely Non-Aggressive	22.0	22.0	153.5	338.0
	Non-Aggressive	73.0	73.0	153.5	338.0
	Neither Non-Aggressive N..	117.0	58.5	153.5	338.0
	Aggressive	111.0	0.0	153.5	338.0
	Extremely Aggressive	15.0	0.0	153.5	338.0
Antonion Dolohov	Extremely Non-Aggressive	1.0	1.0	46.5	333.0
	Non-Aggressive	11.0	11.0	46.5	333.0
	Neither Non-Aggressive N..	69.0	34.5	46.5	333.0
	Aggressive	137.0	0.0	46.5	333.0
	Extremely Aggressive	115.0	0.0	46.5	333.0
Arthur Weasley	Extremely Non-Aggressive	98.0	98.0	288.0	339.0
	Non-Aggressive	146.0	146.0	288.0	339.0
	Neither Non-Aggressive N..	88.0	44.0	288.0	339.0
	Aggressive	7.0	0.0	288.0	339.0

Figure 9.25 This calculated field counts the total number of scores for each question so as to calculate the length of the entire bar.

Calculated Field #4: Gantt Start

The next step is to create a calculated field that will determine the percentage offset, or how far into the negative to begin building the bar chart. Because what we are creating is a modified Gantt chart, this calculated field is really intended to be the first data point in the Gantt chart.

Create this calculated field, named Gantt Start:

−[Total Negative Sentiment]/[Total Sentiment Scores]

Because this number will be expressed as a percentage, we need to adjust the number format. Do this by right-clicking on the measure and choosing Default Properties > Number Format (Figure 9.26). Select Percentage from the menu and enter the number of decimal points.

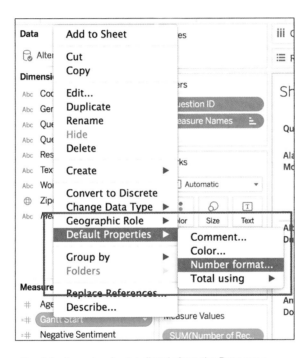

Figure 9.26 Change the default number format directly from the Data pane.

You can spot-check the Gantt Start calculated field after it's added into the crosstab by comparing it against the number of positive and negative responses. The higher the count of negative responses, the larger the Gantt Start percentage will be (Figure 9.27).

Question ID	Text Value	Number of Records	Negative Sentiment	Total Negative Sentiment	Total Sentiment Scores	Gantt Start
Alastor Moody	Extremely Non-Aggressive	1.0	1.0	42.0	338.0	-12.4%
	Non-Aggressive	11.0	11.0	42.0	338.0	-12.4%
	Neither Non-Aggressive N..	60.0	30.0	42.0	338.0	-12.4%
	Aggressive	226.0	0.0	42.0	338.0	-12.4%
	Extremely Aggressive	40.0	0.0	42.0	338.0	-12.4%
Albus Dumbledore	Extremely Non-Aggressive	22.0	22.0	153.5	338.0	-45.4%
	Non-Aggressive	73.0	73.0	153.5	338.0	-45.4%
	Neither Non-Aggressive N..	117.0	58.5	153.5	338.0	-45.4%
	Aggressive	111.0	0.0	153.5	338.0	-45.4%
	Extremely Aggressive	15.0	0.0	153.5	338.0	-45.4%
Antonion Dolohov	Extremely Non-Aggressive	1.0	1.0	46.5	333.0	-14.0%
	Non-Aggressive	11.0	11.0	46.5	333.0	-14.0%
	Neither Non-Aggressive N..	69.0	34.5	46.5	333.0	-14.0%
	Aggressive	137.0	0.0	46.5	333.0	-14.0%
	Extremely Aggressive	115.0	0.0	46.5	333.0	-14.0%

Figure 9.27 The Gantt Start calculated field tells each bar in the Gantt chart where on the axis to begin.

Calculated Field #5: Percent of Gantt Sizing

The next step is to build a calculated field to determine the size of each section of the Gantt chart (i.e., how wide the section should be). Create this calculated field, named Percent of Gantt Sizing:

SUM([Number of Records])/[Total Sentiment Scores]

Again, this is a percentage, so you must adjust the default number format for this calculated field, too.

Calculated Field #6: Gantt Percent Line

The last calculated field tells Tableau where to draw each line after the original Gantt Start data point and separate the sentiment value categories. Create this calculated field, named Gantt Percent Line:

PREVIOUS_VALUE([Gantt Start]) + ZN(LOOKUP([Percent of Total Sizing],−1))

You need to change the default table calculation to Text Values and adjust the default number format to be a percentage.

The Gantt Percent Line is the trickiest of all the calculated fields needed to create the divergent stacked bar chart. Essentially, in plain English, the calculated field begins with the table calculation Previous Value and tells Tableau to look at the previous row of the calculation we've just made. However, there is no previous row for the first line in the table, so we are actually directing Tableau to Gantt Start instead (−12.4%). We then tell Tableau to add the previous row, this time on Percent of Total Sizing, and subtract 1. Again, because there is no previous value, we've directed Tableau to zero nulls (ZN), and the first value in this column is −12.04%. In the next row, we can see this formula begin to work more smoothly (Figure 9.28).

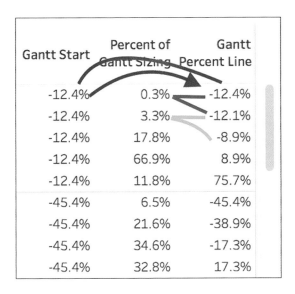

Gantt Start	Percent of Gantt Sizing	Gantt Percent Line
-12.4%	0.3%	-12.4%
-12.4%	3.3%	-12.1%
-12.4%	17.8%	-8.9%
-12.4%	66.9%	8.9%
-12.4%	11.8%	75.7%
-45.4%	6.5%	-45.4%
-45.4%	21.6%	-38.9%
-45.4%	34.6%	-17.3%
-45.4%	32.8%	17.3%

Figure 9.28 The Gantt Percent Line calculated field creates a new calculation using the values generated from previously created calculated fields.

After all five of these new calculated fields have been created and added into the view, the crosstab for the divergent stacked bar chart is complete (Figure 9.29). We are now ready to begin building the visualization in a new sheet.

Question ID	Text Value	Number of Records	Negative Sentiment	Total Negative Sentiment	Total Sentiment Scores	Gantt Start	Percent of Gantt Sizing	Gantt Percent Line
Alastor Moody	Extremely Non-Aggressive	1.0	1.0	42.0	338.0	-12.4%	0.3%	-12.4%
	Non-Aggressive	11.0	11.0	42.0	338.0	-12.4%	3.3%	-12.1%
	Neither Non-Aggressive N...	60.0	30.0	42.0	338.0	-12.4%	17.8%	-8.9%
	Aggressive	226.0	0.0	42.0	338.0	-12.4%	66.9%	8.9%
	Extremely Aggressive	40.0	0.0	42.0	338.0	-12.4%	11.8%	75.7%
Albus Dumbledore	Extremely Non-Aggressive	22.0	22.0	153.5	338.0	-45.4%	6.5%	-45.4%
	Non-Aggressive	73.0	73.0	153.5	338.0	-45.4%	21.6%	-38.9%
	Neither Non-Aggressive N...	117.0	58.5	153.5	338.0	-45.4%	34.6%	-17.3%
	Aggressive	111.0	0.0	153.5	338.0	-45.4%	32.8%	17.3%
	Extremely Aggressive	15.0	0.0	153.5	338.0	-45.4%	4.4%	50.1%
Antonin Dolohov	Extremely Non-Aggressive	1.0	1.0	46.5	333.0	-14.0%	0.3%	-14.0%
	Non-Aggressive	11.0	11.0	46.5	333.0	-14.0%	3.3%	-13.7%
	Neither Non-Aggressive N...	69.0	34.5	46.5	333.0	-14.0%	20.7%	-10.4%
	Aggressive	137.0	0.0	46.5	333.0	-14.0%	41.1%	10.4%
	Extremely Aggressive	115.0	0.0	46.5	333.0	-14.0%	34.5%	51.5%
Arthur Weasley	Extremely Non-Aggressive	98.0	98.0	298.0	339.0	-85.0%	28.9%	-85.0%
	Non-Aggressive	146.0	146.0	298.0	339.0	-85.0%	43.1%	-56.0%
	Neither Non-Aggressive N...	88.0	44.0	298.0	339.0	-85.0%	26.0%	-13.0%
	Aggressive	7.0	0.0	298.0	339.0	-85.0%	2.1%	13.0%
Barty Crouch	Extremely Non-Aggressive	2.0	2.0	33.0	337.0	-9.8%	0.6%	-9.8%

Figure 9.29 Although it's a long process, this crosstab creates the foundation for our eventual Likert-scale visualization.

In a new sheet, drag the Question dimension to the Rows shelf and the Gantt Percent Line measure to the Columns shelf. ***Tableau will break immediately***, flagging the measure in red and giving the error message that a critical field used to create this calculation is missing from the view (Figure 9.30).

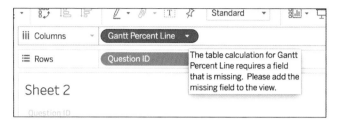

Figure 9.30 The first step in creating this Likert-scale visualization throws an error—but that's okay!

The missing field is Text Value, which is the field we calculated everything over in the crosstab. Bring this dimension into the view and drop it on the Color Marks card. You might need to filter and then add the dimension, depending on how many options it has.

Immediately we see a divergent stacked bar chart begin to appear! However, as we're actually creating a Gantt chart, we still have quite a bit of work to do:

1. Change the mark from Automatic to Gantt Bar (Figure 9.31). This adjusts the view from bars to lines that separate each section of the Gantt chart.

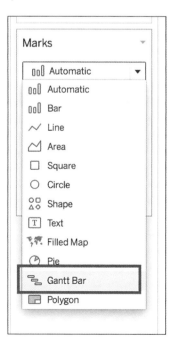

Figure 9.31 Changing the mark from the automatic bar to a Gantt bar begins the Gantt chart transformation.

2. You need to manually re-sort your text value options in the same way we discussed when making the crosstab table. This time, however, click the Sort option on the Color Marks card and manually adjust it so that text values display in the correct ranking order (minimum to maximum, or 1 to 5).

3. Drag and drop the Percent of Gantt Sizing calculated field on the Size Marks card. Now, the visualization is beginning to take shape.

4. Now to address color: Tableau has used the automatic color palette, which is intended to make things look very different. For this example, we'll make the colors look more like a standard blue–orange diverging palette by changing the colors to a colorblind palette and manually selecting better color choices (Figure 9.32).

   Because this scale is from "extremely non-aggressive" to "extremely aggressive," I used color choices that reflect the severity of character aggression. You could use other color scales depending on the context of the story and the takeaway intended.

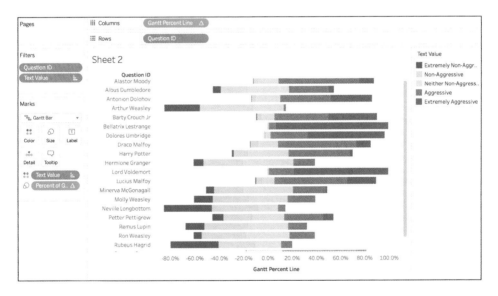

Figure 9.32 With a few quick clicks, and by leveraging the calculated fields already made and making smart color choices, the divergent chart is beginning to take shape.

5. Now, to fix the axis: Because we know that the axis can range from –1 to 1, adjust it by right-clicking on the *x*-axis, selecting Edit Axis, and then changing the fixed range from –1 to 1 (Figure 9.33). This shifts the bars slightly so that everything is centered on the zero midpoint.

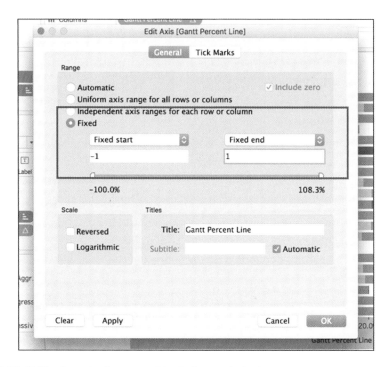

Figure 9.33 Shifting the axis allows everything to line up nicely at zero.

A few more clicks to simplify and remove headers and clean up the visualization delivers a stunning divergent bar chart that displays the Likert-scale sentiment data nicely. (The final result will look like Figure 9.20, shown earlier in the chapter.)

Lollipop Charts

While not native to Tableau, the lollipop chart is a hybrid chart that combines a traditional bar chart and a Cleveland dot plot. It is simply a dual-axis chart that superimposes a circle on top of a very thin bar chart (Figure 9.34). However, it's a fun way to spice up a bar chart to give it more visual appeal without reducing its analytical integrity.

> **note**
>
> Lollipop charts are a helpful way to visualize many bars of the same length while avoiding the moiré effect. This exercise uses the Baby Names dataset, which is available in the Tableau dataset library at https://public.tableau.com/app/resources/sample-data. This dataset contains the most popular male and female names in each state for each year from 1910 to 2012, based on data collected by the Social Security Administration.

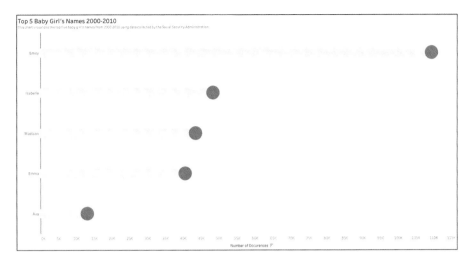

Figure 9.34 Completed lollipop chart.

A lollipop chart is a great choice for comparing multiple measures because it helps the reader to align categories to points without drowning the graphic in ink. It typically contains categorical variables on the *y*-axis measured against a second (continuous) variable on the *x*-axis, although these can also be plotted on the *y*-axis. With either orientation, the emphasis is on the circle, as it is a visual cue to draw the audience's attention to the specific value in each category. The line (or bar) itself is meant to be a minimalistic approach to tie each category to its relative point without drawing too much attention to the line itself.

To begin:

1. Build a basic bar chart in Tableau (Figure 9.35). Here, I have filtered the dataset to include only girls' names from 2000 to 2010.

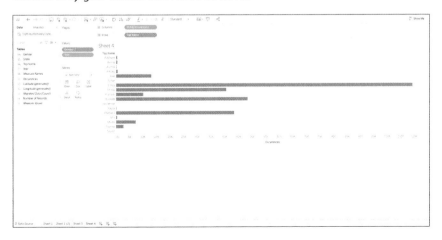

Figure 9.35 Begin with a basic bar chart.

2. Duplicate your dimension on the same shelf you are currently using to display dimensions (in this example, the Columns shelf). This creates a side-by-side view of two identical bar charts (Figure 9.36).

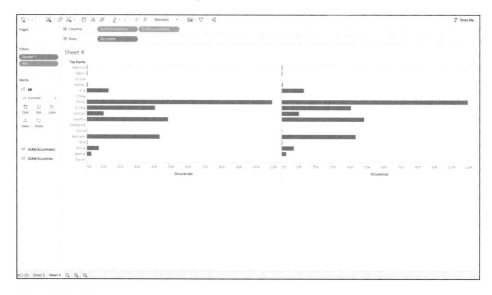

Figure 9.36 A little messy at first, duplicating your dimension creates a side-by-side view of two identical bar charts.

3. Using the duplicated measure, adjust to a dual axis by right-clicking the second measure (or second axis) and selecting Dual Axis (Figure 9.37). Because the mark Type is set to Automatic, Tableau will likely convert both visualizations to circle charts.

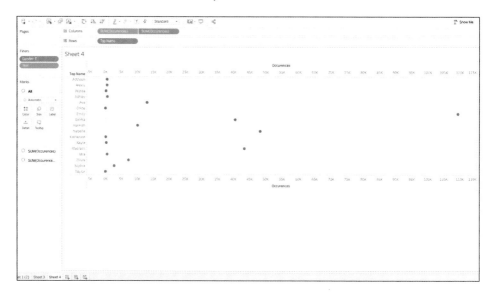

Figure 9.37 Converting to a dual axis adjusts the marks, but you can now change the Marks formatting for each dimension.

4. Using the Marks card, change the first occurrence of your dimension to a bar. Use the Size slider to slim down the line and the Color Marks to adjust the color of the bar as appropriate. I typically use a lighter gray (Figure 9.38).

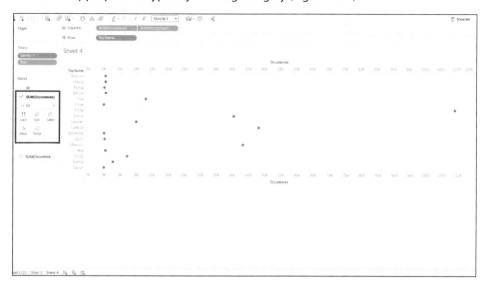

Figure 9.38 With your first marks adjustment, the lollipop charts begins to take shape.

5. To adjust the second dimension occurrence, using the Size Marks card, enlarge the circles as appropriate (Figure 9.39).

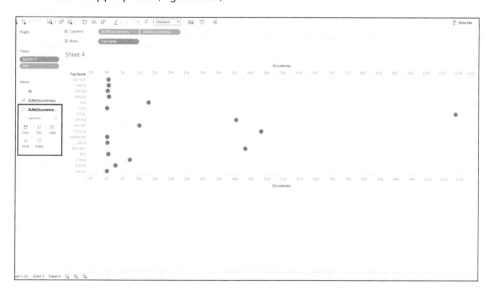

Figure 9.39 The bars and circles of the lollipop chart can be changed individually in terms of their size and color to curate your chart.

With the basis of the lollipop chart built, it's time to clean up the visualization.

6. Make sure your axes line up correctly. Right-click the second measure axis (the one on top) and choose Synchronize Axis to make the axes equal. Right-click the axis again and uncheck Show Header.

7. Tidy up the visual by sorting bars and excluding any data that might not be pertinent to your story. I have sorted in Descending order and excluded everything but the top 5 names. (You will need to readjust the Marks Sizing after this step.)

8. Continue removing headers and axis titles as well as adjusting titles as appropriate until you are happy with the visualization.

Labeled Lollipops

You might elect to remove the bottom axis header and use the circles to encode their value.

To do this, drag the measure to the canvas for a third time, this time dropping it on the Label card on the second occurrence. Adjust the Label alignment to be centered and Automatic, and make sure the check box to allow marks to overlap other labels is selected (Figure 9.40).

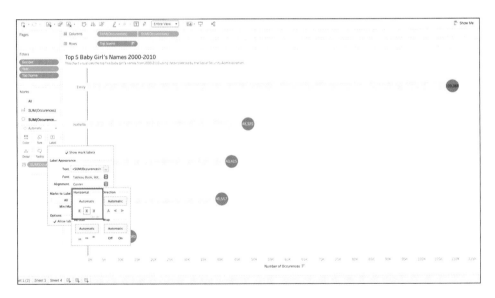

Figure 9.40 Carefully formatting mark labels can embed additional data in your lollipop chart and eliminate the need for axis headers.

Right-click on the dimension on the Labels shelf to format the number and text color, and then remove axis headers and tweak as necessary (Figure 9.41).

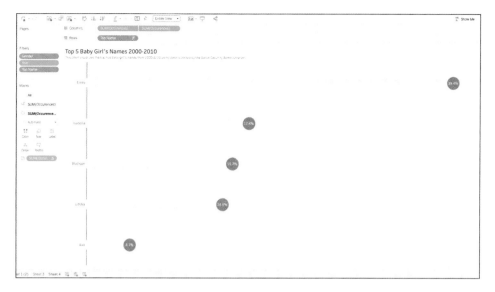

Figure 9.41 With proper size, color, and label adjustments, a lollipop chart can be a richer visual alternative to a classic bar chart.

Other options to embellish your lollipop charts include color-coding the circles based on a measure or changing circles to custom shapes.

Word Clouds

A word cloud is an image composed of words in which the size of each word indicates its frequency or importance (Figure 9.42). While not particularly analytically astute and not recommended for analytical purposes, these types of visualizations can be a powerful way to display textual data and can be an attention-grabbing technique for the purpose of data storytelling and visual impact. In fact, word clouds can make great bookends to presentations to incite interest or leave a lasting impression on an audience. The good news is that word clouds are quick and simple to create in Tableau.

> note
>
> For this word cloud, I'm using a unigram list of the entire manuscript of *Harry Potter and the Philosopher's Stone*. It's a tremendously large dataset, so I've manually curated a list of keywords to use in this exercise.

Creating a word cloud in Tableau essentially requires using your Text dimension in a variety of marks. First, on a blank canvas, drag the desired dimension to the Text Marks card, and then drag the same dimension to the Size Marks card. At this point your canvas should look similar to Figure 9.43, displaying a simple list of your words in increasingly larger size. Depending on the number of words in your list, this size differential may be more immediately noticeable.

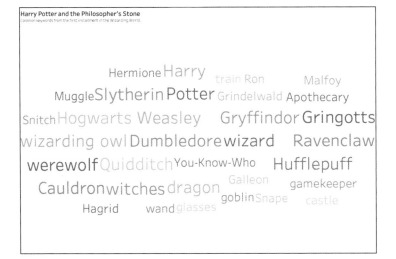

Figure 9.42 A word count of popular Harry Potter keywords created in Tableau.

Figure 9.43 After two quick clicks on the canvas, the structure of a word cloud begins to form.

At this point, you are ready to transform this view into something that better resembles your expectation of a word cloud. To do this, right-click on the dimension on the Size card and select Measure > Count (Figure 9.44).

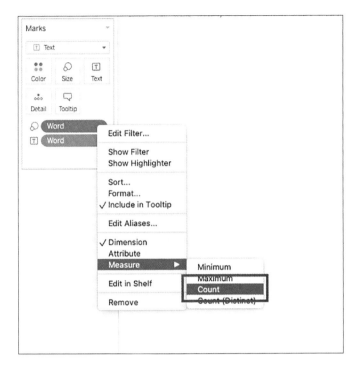

Figure 9.44 Adjust the dimension to a measure to resize the words based on their count.

This step converts your initial word cloud structure to something that looks like a tree map of a single color. Change the Mark type from Automatic to Text, and your word cloud will re-form (Figure 9.45).

Figure 9.45 Changing the Mark type from Automatic to Text reshapes the tree map into something more akin to a word cloud.

You might need to do some additional work to clean up your word cloud, including removing extraneous words, performing deduplication, or streamlining the words included. To add color to the word cloud, drag the text measure once more to the Color Marks card. Now, with a little bit of formatting clean up, your word cloud is complete (Figure 9.46).

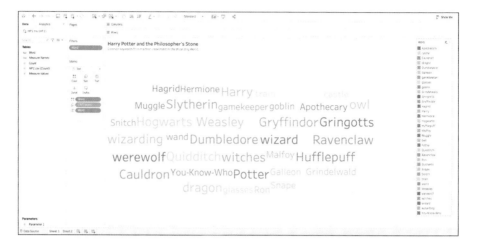

Figure 9.46 To finish your word cloud, add color.

Summary

This chapter described ways to create a few advanced visualizations beyond the fundamental data visualizations available on the Show Me card in Tableau. These charts require a little more hands-on manipulation but can be excellent candidates to add some variety to your dashboards and visual presentations. Aside from the types explored here, many other advanced charts can be built in Tableau. Some fun ones to try on your own might be waffle charts or hexbin map charts, or you can explore the use of spark lines. There are always more charts to learn—so explore and have fun!

CHAPTER 10

CLOSING THOUGHTS

We've covered a lot of ground in this book—
from understanding the value of visual
analytics to putting it into practice to curate
data visualizations and structure compelling
visual data stories using the basic and selected
advanced charts and graphs available in
Tableau.

The lessons in this book are a huge step in the right direction, but they're just the first step. Becoming a seasoned visual analyst takes time. As Neil DeGrasse Tyson says, "As the area of your knowledge grows, so too does the perimeter of your ignorance." We never know everything; we can only keep learning more.

The best visual data analysts recognize that learning how to apply fundamental data visualization best practices and tell meaningful, effective data stories is a skill learned over time with practice, experience, and a good amount of trial and error. These practices are ever-evolving, spurred onward by the advent of technologies and by inspiring, innovative analysts and artists who have the courage and curiosity to experiment with new approaches and new ideas. It's important that we, as visual analysts, data explorers, and storytellers, commit to continuous learning, both with visualization and with tools, in Tableau and beyond, as new capabilities are introduced that facilitate deeper visual analysis.

In that spirit, this final chapter recaps the main lessons covered throughout the text. It also serves as a resource kit for life beyond the book by providing checklists of best practices and practical suggestions for continuing to master outputs of visual analytics. In addition, it discusses the myriad resources available to support you on this journey.

Five Steps to Visual Data Storytelling

In his book *Data Points: Visualization That Means Something*, statistician and data visualization expert Nathan Yau notes that today's visual data stories are "something in-between the textbook and the novel." Today's visual narratives combine skills of computer science, statistics, artistic design, and storytelling.

Here are five steps to guide you as you work to build a perfect data story.

Step 1. Find Data That Supports Your Story

Whether you're crafting a data visualization or a data story, the first step in creating your data narrative is to find (or collect) data that supports the story you want to tell. The storytelling process is, in many ways, more similar to the scientific process than to any literary one. After all, as a visual analyst and storyteller, you are tasked with asking questions, performing background research, constructing and testing one or many hypotheses, and analyzing information to draw a conclusion.

As we've seen throughout this text, finding data to support a story doesn't necessarily require researching scientific data. Ultimately, the data chosen should support the story it is telling in context, complexity, and depth. In other words, find a story you're interested in telling. Then, make sure you understand your data and respect its limitations, knowing which story your data *can* logically support and where you might need to incorporate additional data to fill gaps or answer important questions.

Step 2. Layer Information for Understanding

After you have the goals of your data in hand and its story clearly in mind, script your story by layering information to build a framework around a narrative. Plotting a clear beginning, middle, and end, as well as a clear message, will ensure the narrative fits your audience's needs. In writing terms, think of this as constructing your story's outline and plot.

Remember, knowledge is incremental. Every piece of information we learn is founded on something we already know. Thus, layering information is critical: It's a tool you can use to guide your audience as a narrator, first by providing a foundation for learning, and then by building upon this with additional information. In data storytelling, you can achieve this goal by compounding builds in visualization or sequencing different types of visualizations, providing annotations or interactive capabilities on a dashboard, drilling deeper into a single visualization, and so on.

Step 3. Design to Reveal

Charts can't do it all. As tools to communicate insights, data visualizations can't be relied upon to tell the whole story for you. Likewise, various types of visualization can present the data properly, but still fail to tell a story. Thus, you should choose your data and your visual form so that the two work in tandem while communicating a single accurate and meaningful message. Then, put the right dialogue into place—whether through narration or embedded into a visualization—to guide your audience through your story.

Start by stripping out unnecessary information and focusing on the most powerful elements and takeaways. At the same time, recognize that these aren't always the most obvious trends or elements. And remember: There is not always one truth in data—and that's where context becomes a critical element of a data story.

Step 4. Beware the False Reveal

A false reveal can be a dangerous thing. It can incite the audience to draw the wrong conclusions or take an incorrect action. It can also damage the effect of the data itself and your credibility as a storyteller. As a visual data documentary, data stories should be engaging and entertaining, but should focus foremost on sharing truths.

Whether we do it intentionally or inadvertently, we can force the data to tell the story we want it to, even if it's the wrong—or an inaccurate—one. With visual narratives, we are tasked not only with telling a story, but also making it interesting, engaging, and inspiring. Think of a visual story as a documentary: a nonfiction work, based on a collection of data, told in a visually compelling way.

Step 5. Tell It Fast

Stories have an inherent amount of entropy and are most potent when they are happening. Data journalists take this point to heart in models that keep track of events as they happen in real time (e.g., political elections or disaster scenarios). The timestamp on when data is reported (or a visualization or visual story released) can make a big difference in how the story is interpreted or what impact it makes.

One way to tell a data story fast is by sharing it through mobile channels. Mobile devices have been a game changer for data visualization in many ways and will likely become even more important in the years ahead. That said, mobile presentations require wise editing. Be aware of form factor limitations and rethink the way storytelling via mobile devices happens.

The Important Role of Feedback

Back in my industry years, I developed and brought to market a concept called the Data Visualization Competency Center (DVCC). At its heart, this methodology described the framework for a permanent, formal organizational structure tasked with advancing and promoting the effective use of data visualization as an information asset within the business.

One of the most imperative tenets of the DVCC is the need for feedback. As with any type of analytics, visual analytics and visualization outputs that are created and used in isolation can become their own version of data silos. We should not overlook the need to collaborate and engage in group critiques before publishing new visuals or presenting new data stories.

Successful data visualizations should be able to be understood by the intended audience from a position of personal insight and experience—that is, the visualization should tell a meaningful story. Collaboration helps ensure the visualization does tell a story, particularly the one the author anticipated it would tell.

The need for feedback is applicable both at an organizational level and at an individual level. All visual analysts should user-test their visualizations and stories to ensure the message they are working to communicate is the same one being received by their intended audience. Here are a few ways to test the usability of your visualization:

- Give a mock presentation to colleagues or friends to confirm that they "see" the same insights you do.
- Ask a member of your intended audience if they can explain the message in the visualization.
- Have someone get hands-on with your visualization and see whether they can navigate its filters, actions, or annotations.

Frankly, the process of user-testing a data visualization or story is easier said than done, and feedback can be a fickle friend. We invest a significant amount of time and energy into building visualizations and crafting narratives, and, as with any creation, we become attached to them—and perhaps somewhat blind to their potential flaws. Even so, feedback can be validating or constructive, and if collected consciously can help us engage audiences and perfect our data stories.

The old phrase "Everyone's a critic" is alive and well in visual analytics. I've created many visualizations that have not been as brilliant as I thought they were. Tableau guru Steve Wexler, in his blog *Data Revelations*, expressed a similar sentiment, even describing the moments of anger or depression that can accompany less than enthusiastic feedback about a new visualization. Being resistant to or wary of feedback is *normal*. Instead of dwelling on negative feedback, use it as an impetus to improve your visualization, engage in corrective learning, and seek out new information to add into your visual data storytelling skillset for your next project.

> note
>
> For more on the Data Visualization Competency Center, check out the Visual Imperative or the whitepaper from Radiant Advisors, available at https://radiantadvisors.com/our-research/new-research-the-data-visualization-competency-center.

Ongoing Learning

Practice and receiving audience feedback are important ways to continuously learn and perfect your skills as a visual analyst, visualization designer, and data storyteller. Many additional resources—both those that accompany this text and those you can find out in the wild—are available to aid you in ongoing training and skills development.

Teach Yourself: External Resources

A bevy of incredible information assets beyond this book can expand and deepen your knowledge and understanding of the concepts we approached from a pragmatic stance in this text. The following are some of the resources I recommend.

Blogs

Blogs have two great qualities: There are a lot of them, and they are constantly adding new material and new ideas. Here are a few of my favorites that offer unique and compelling galleries of visual data storytelling in action, created by some of the most prominent voices in data visualization and storytelling today.

- **Flowing Data** (http://flowingdata.com): This blog, run by data visualization author and statistician Nathan Yau, explores how we can use analysis, visualization, and exploration to understand data and ourselves.

- **Storytelling with Data** (www.storytellingwithdata.com/blog): This blog, run by visualization expert Cole Nussbaumer Knaflic, exists to help visual analysts create compelling narratives, making this site an "online destination for practicing and honing data visualization and storytelling skills."

- **Eager Eyes** (https://eagereyes.org): This blog devoted to visualization and visual communication belongs to Tableau research lead Robert Kosara. It explores what we know and what we don't know—so we can be less wrong about visualization.

- **The Pudding** (https://pudding.cool): *The Pudding* is a weekly journal of visual essays produced by Polygraph (http://polygraph.cool), an "incubator for visually driven storytelling." Using code, animation, and data visualization, these stories tackle a wide range of interesting topic matter, including insights from politics, cinema and art, and science.

- **Info We Trust** (http://infowetrust.com): This website belongs to RJ Andrews, an independent creative whose visualizations provide a striking lesson in how to use design and science to humanize complex information using analysis, illustration, motion, and interactive design.

- **Bora Beran "On Anything Data"** (https://boraberan.wordpress.com): This site, which belongs to Tableau's Bora Beran, takes a unique look at more technical aspects of data visualization, including building extremely complex visuals, such as sunburst diagrams, in Tableau, and using languages like R and Python to collect and prepare data for visual analysis.

- **Data Revelations** (www.datarevelations.com): Run by Tableau Zen master and training partner Steve Wexler, this blog provides practical training and hands-on guidance on using Tableau to properly and creatively visualize data.

- **Information Is Beautiful** (www.informationisbeautiful.net): This blog by data journalist David McCandless, focuses on distilling the world's data, information, and knowledge into beautiful and useful graphics to help everyone make better, clearer, more informed decisions about the world.

Books

Many books, both old and new, take deep dives into many of the concepts covered in this book, as well as provide valuable insights from other leading voices in the field. Several of these books are Tableau specific, providing more practicable learning to apply concepts and test your skills. Here are a few of the titles I use as references, both in and out of my classroom:

- *The Visual Imperative: Creating a Visual Culture of Data Discovery* by Lindy Ryan
- *Storytelling with Data: A Data Visualization Guide for Business Professionals* by Cole Nussbaumer Knaflic
- *The Functional Art: An Introduction to Information Graphics and Visualization (Voices That Matter)* by Alberto Cairo
- *Data Points: Visualization That Means Something* by Nathan Yau
- *Communicating Data with Tableau: Designing, Developing, and Delivering Data Visualizations* by Ben Jones
- *Tableau Your Data!: Fast and Easy Visual Analysis with Tableau Software* by Daniel Murray
- *Visual Analytics with Tableau* by Alexander Loth
- *DataStory: Explain Data and Inspire Action Through Story* by Nancy Duarte
- *Practical Tableau: 100 Tips, Tutorials, and Strategies from a Tableau Zen Master* by Ryan Sleeper
- *Visual Analysis and Design* by Tamara Munzner

Tableau Resources

Tableau has a rich and expansive set of resources, including blogs, whitepapers, visualization galleries, webinars, training videos, and more, that are available to the general public either free or for a fee. Additionally, educators and students can access relevant, in-depth materials, including datasets, through Tableau's community forums and special interest groups.

Resources offered by Tableau are included in both the Introduction and Appendix A, "Tableau Services."

Companion Materials to This Text

Alongside the external resources outlined previously, there are several companion materials designed to accompany this text to provide additional hands-on support for practitioners and educators. These are available to you at no additional cost, and are freely available online:

- **Website** (http://www.lindyryanwrites.com/academic): This website acts as an information hub to share all companion materials, including lecture decks, datasets, and more.
- **Datasets:** All publicly available datasets used in this text are available either from their original source or through http://www.lindyryanwrites.com. Additionally, Tableau catalogs a wide array of datasets that can be used to practice, teach, or otherwise engage with data visualization.
- **Curricula:** Designed for entry to mid-level analysts, as well as undergraduate and graduate students, selected lecture materials and assignments to support this text are also available. These are hosted and available via Pearson Education for educators. They are incrementally updated and include recommended readings and videos. Guest lecturing services are available to university faculty, as well as corporate training workshops for industry professionals. Tableau also offers educator support with its Tableau for Teaching program, which includes classroom software licensing and curricula kits.
- **Connect with me:** Reach out to me directly on any social media. I love to engage with you and see what stories you are telling with data!
  - **Twitter:** @lindyryanwrites
  - **Tableau Public:** https://public.tableau.com/app/profile/lindy.ryan
  - **LinkedIn:** www.linkedin.com/in/lindyryan/

TABLEAU SERVICES

Tableau offers several solutions designed to help users continue to grow and improve as visual data analysts within the Tableau ecosystem. While there are additional learning paths available for organizations, we'll focus on those offerings that support individual learners.

eLearning

Tableau eLearning provides web-based trainings that users can consume at their own pace. Varied in length and skill level, these interactive learning experiences are designed to help users grow in efficacy with Tableau. New lessons are added regularly, making eLearning a trusted resource to get the most up-to-date Tableau training content.

Through a combination of curated curriculum, metric-based skill assessments, and gamification via digital badges, role-based learning paths provide the option for users to engage in training directly related to their role in an organization or their learning priorities (Figure A.1).

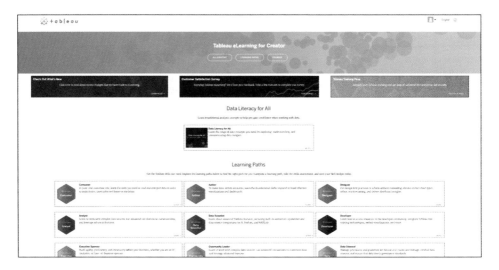

Figure A.1 The Tableau eLearning environment

Instructor-Led Training

Tableau's comprehensive instructor-led training—which can be delivered privately or publicly, in person or online—provides learning support for Tableau Desktop, Tableau Server, and Tableau Prep. It combines trainer expertise and hands-on activities to help learners practice skills learned in a pedagogical environment.

Tableau Help

Tableau Help is a comprehensive resource in which users can find answers to many questions through Tableau Knowledge Base articles and documentation access via Tableau's website. Resources include training videos, whitepapers, and more and are accessible at help.tableau.com as well as directly from within the Tableau product environment (Figure A.2).

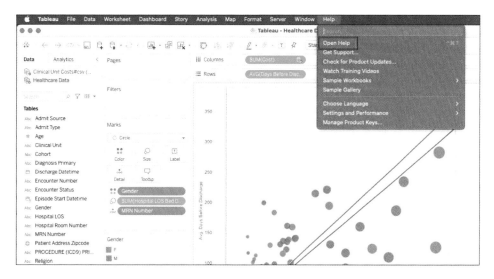

Figure A.2 Accessing Tableau Help from within Tableau Desktop.

Tableau Community

Connect to thousands of Tableau users for help, support, or inspiration in a robust online community. The Tableau Community is an active, engaged network of visualization professionals that supports forums, feature requests, groups, events, and resources including workbooks and other options. Join at community.tableau.com.

Tableau Knowledge Base

The Tableau Knowledge Base (KB) is an ever-expanding library of solutions to common questions provided by the Tableau support team. These resources are compiled from various Tableau assets and include a search engine to help you quickly and easily locate the answers you need. Access the Knowledge Base at kb.tableau.com.

INDEX

Photo by Marvent/Shutterstock

VIDEO TRAINING FOR THE **IT PROFESSIONAL**

LEARN QUICKLY
Learn a new technology in just hours. Video training can teach more in less time, and material is generally easier to absorb and remember.

WATCH AND LEARN
Instructors demonstrate concepts so you see technology in action.

TEST YOURSELF
Our Complete Video Courses offer self-assessment quizzes throughout.

CONVENIENT
Most videos are streaming with an option to download lessons for offline viewing.

Learn more, browse our store, and watch free, sample lessons at
informit.com/video

Save 50%* off the list price of video courses with discount code **VIDBOB**

Register Your Product at informit.com/register

Access additional benefits and save up to 65%* on your next purchase

- Automatically receive a coupon for 35% off books, eBooks, and web editions and 65% off video courses, valid for 30 days. Look for your code in your InformIT cart or the Manage Codes section of your account page.
- Download available product updates.
- Access bonus material if available.**
- Check the box to hear from us and receive exclusive offers on new editions and related products.

InformIT—The Trusted Technology Learning Source

InformIT is the online home of information technology brands at Pearson, the world's leading learning company. At informit.com, you can

- Shop our books, eBooks, and video training. Most eBooks are DRM-Free and include PDF and EPUB files.
- Take advantage of our special offers and promotions (informit.com/promotions).
- Sign up for special offers and content newsletter (informit.com/newsletters).
- Access thousands of free chapters and video lessons.
- Enjoy free ground shipping on U.S. orders.*

* Offers subject to change.
** Registration benefits vary by product. Benefits will be listed on your account page under Registered Products.

Connect with InformIT—Visit informit.com/community

 twitter.com/informit

 Pearson

Addison-Wesley • Adobe Press • Cisco Press • Microsoft Press • Oracle Press • Peachpit Press • Pearson IT Certification • Que